Nurturing My Nest

Nurturing My Nest

Intentional Homebuilding Ideas
& Custom Built Homeschooling

Leah Vance Simpson

ISBN: 153972736X
ISBN: -13: 9781539727361
Library of Congress Control Number: 2016920964
CreateSpace Independent Publishing Platform
North Charleston, South Carolina

Praise for *Nurturing My Nest*

"In *Nurturing My Nest*, Leah Simpson shares from her wealth of experience and expertise in all areas of the home. I have known Leah for many years and have admired how intentional and engaged she is with her family. She and Tim and their five children have created a warm and hospitable home where guests feel welcome and look forward to being invited back. I am drawn to her gracious spirit and genuine walk with Christ. I recommend her book to all young mothers who long to "train up their children in the way they should go" (Ps. 22:6). *Nurturing My Nest* will give you great ideas and suggestions for education, home organization, meal planning and so much more! In our over committed culture that seems to be pulling families apart, Leah gives us a tool for rediscovering the power and importance of the Christian home. This treasure is a guide no homeschooling parent should be without!"

- **Donna Gaines** is a speaker, author of *Seated: Living from Our Position in Christ* and *Leaving Ordinary: Encounter God Through Prayer* and founder of Arise2Read, a nonprofit that recruits churches and businesses to adopt and provide tutors for inner-city elementary schools. Donna also teaches Bible studies at her home church, Bellevue Baptist Church, in the Memphis Area where her husband, Steve Gaines, Southern Baptist Convention President, pastors.

Nurturing My Nest is a refreshing look at the ins and outs of homeschooling from a mother who is a master at designing a curriculum to fit the unique giftedness of the whole child. The product of a homeschool education herself, Leah has not only created individual programs for each of her five children, but she has also taught countless others to do so as well. In this comprehensive handbook, you will find helpful insights, practical ideas, and spiritual encouragement to support you in your homeschool journey. "Nurturing My Nest" is sure to become a treasured resource in your library.

- **Dayna Street,** Women's Ministry Director at Bellevue Baptist Church

This book is dedicated to my parents, my husband and my five beautiful children.

My parents, Bob and Aloha Vance, have served God on the mission field for over sixty years. My childhood was one of adventure and happiness. They emphasized that they were not the missionaries, but that we were all privileged to serve God together as a team. Because of this vision, I grew up learning numerous ways to serve the Lord practically among unreached people. My childhood was spent in St. Lucia, West Indies and the Big Island of Hawaii. I am grateful that I was included on their missionary journeys. I am thankful that I was homeschooled many of those years. I am immensely appreciative for the deep, abiding love for the Lord that enveloped me early. For all the wonderful things you did to nurture our home, Mom and Dad, I thank you! This book is so much a reflection of what you demonstrated in the home where I grew up.

Mom & Dad - December 2014

This book is also dedicated to my loving husband of nearly thirty years. Together we have created a loving, Godly home where all five of our children know two parents who love them. Knowing God personally and living a life to glorify Him is the message we aim to live out together.

To my husband: There was an instant attraction to you. I love you for so many reasons. With unexpected enthusiasm, I know that I love you more than I did on the day we married. Thank you for being the rock, the alpha male, the stud, the steady, the funny, the faithful, the loving, the patient, the calm, and the encourager. You are a good man.

Us at Katie's wedding. One of the happiest days of our lives.

To my five children who are truly gifts from God, much of this book is a story about you. You are God's gifts to us. Your daddy and I prayed for each of you. Along the journey we lost six little ones through miscarriage, so maybe this caused us to hold you each tighter. I have loved homeschooling because it has given us the blessing of being with you through so much of your childhood. You have been given our very best. For all the memories, I am so grateful! You are dearly loved. Your daddy and I are so very proud of each of you.

Simpson kids in Kona, Hawaii 2015

Contents

Introduction

Truthfully, my husband persuaded me to write this book. I feel that the ideas in these pages may be common to many of you. I am really just a simple girl blessed beyond words. As a mother of five beautiful children, a grateful wife, a sister, a daughter, a friend, a teacher, a servant, and a follower of Jesus Christ, I stand humbled. My daily work consists primarily of physically caring for my family and schooling my children. For those of you in the trenches, you recognize the never-ending schedule. So, embarking on this project amid all my other responsibilities seemed daunting.

My life is far from perfect, but I am deeply blessed. Like all moms, I have dreams for my life as a mother and for my family. As life unfolds, our expectations can be thwarted, and we can be disappointed. Because we cannot see the future, it is always hard to formulate the next decision. I am not perfect. My children are not perfect. My house is not perfect. Even though I have been homeschooling for twenty-two years, taught classes in private school and homeschool tutorials and successfully graduated three students from homeschooling, one of my children was recently educated at first a private school and then a public school. All that said, not all children fit nicely into homeschooling, and not all parents are right for homeschooling. This book is more about the whole child than it is about homeschooling. It is about nurturing our homes rather than having a perfect one. It is full of hope and inspiration instead of presumptions.

This book is my gift to you, the reader, on your journey of parenting and homeschooling. Many are raising children as single parents and stay-at-home dads. These ideas work for any intentional and caring parent. Whether you are brand new or seasoned in your quest, I pray you will find inspiration for your home. Although this book is geared toward homeschooling families, about a third of it offers ideas that can be implemented in any home. For those of you who parent alone, my heart reaches out to you with great compassion. May these words offer you courage as well as encouragement.

This handbook is not really intended to be read from front to back. This is good to know if you are like me. I always start at the beginning and read straight through without peeking ahead. Study the chapter titles, and read the chapters that appeal to you or answer your current concerns. New moms should start with chapter 1. Even though I have been schooling for more than twenty years, I still gather up homeschool help books, eager to find a gem, an idea, or a treasure. So jump in where you deem best.

Family at Katie & Zach's wedding

Now entering my twenty-second year as a homeschooling mom, I am beginning to look up from this intensive daily task. My oldest just graduated from college. With his ACT score of 33, he earned a full academic scholarship to college and just completed his last semester with a 3.67 grade-point average (GPA). The remaining four children were born within five years. Two of them are in college, while the younger two are in high school. In many ways, these four were parented and schooled in pairs. The girls and the boys were born eighteen months apart. The girls are now serious about their college years, working diligently. When they were in high school, the days swirled around academics, speech and debate competitions, their business, musical instruments, and spending time with friends. My young boys, who resist being called little boys, left their elementary years for the emotion and swagger of junior high. Now suddenly in high school, they enjoy some school, sports, speech and debate, new friends, and time with Dad.

As I reflect on this junction in my life, I remember back to a day when my husband and I had no children. The future reality of having a family seemed bleak. Our hopes of having a family began with the expectation of twins. Shortly after falling in love with them during our first sonogram, they were gone. Such unexpected and overwhelming sorrow engulfed us. We prayed. We wept. We hoped. Before long, our oldest son was born. Words cannot express the joy of those days. In the years that followed, we miscarried five more babies. I wondered if we would have an only child. We prayed specifically for just one more so that we could have a bigger family. Miraculously, after all this heartache, we were blessed with four children in five years. I think the success of having children after such difficulty left me clinging to them too tightly.

I am reminded daily that children are on loan from God. In these years of releasing them to adulthood, I remind myself of this generous loan from God. He blessed us with the opportunity to enjoy them, to train them, and to watch them grow. Through all the heartache as well as the joy, I lift my hands in thanksgiving for the life God called me to live as their mother. I'm often reminded of Gretchen Rubin's words: "The days are long, but the years are short." How true!

My story began as the oldest child of two ambitious young people. My parents met in college while taking an Old Testament survey class. My father informs us that, although he was very interested in studying the Old Testament, he instead found himself survey-ing a fellow student, my mother. Curious about my mother's un-usual name, Aloha, he asked its meaning.

She responded, "It means *hello.*"

He thought, *Well…hello.*

Then she said, "It also means *goodbye.*"

To that he responded, "Oh dear."

Finally, she said, "It also means *I love you.*"

So, that is how it all started. My father, a new Christian in his mid-twenties, married my mother, who was raised in the church. Both desired to spend their lives in full-time Christian service. This passion drew them together on a life journey.

Bob, Aloha, Leah, Nathan and Daphne Vance
in St. Lucia, West Indies circa 1973

Fast forward a few years past their college graduation, marriage, and missionary deputation. As rookie missionaries on their way to the West Indies, my parents paused in the United States to have their first child. When I was six months old, my parents and I left on our first adventure as a missionary family headed for the tiny island of Saint Lucia in the West Indies. Now, more than fifty years later, my parents still serve as missionaries. Today, I spoke with my mother as they were serving as short-term replacements for missionaries in Canada. Over the years they have served in Saint Lucia, West Indies; the big island of Hawaii; and Canada. In their "retirement," they work in mission relief, counseling, and teaching. So, my heritage is rich in family and Christian service.

I am pictured with our London taxi in St. Lucia, West Indies

My oldest son has recently finished college and begun a new phase of what they all now call "adulting." This change prompted him to show his sister a very clean room. She asked where her brother had gone, since this behavior seemed unusual for him. He completed college with an internship thrown in just for fun. This spring he helped with a mission trip to India and the Dominican Republic. Life is moving faster. I enjoy watching him grow.

Recently, I watched my oldest daughter teach her Sunday school class of three-year-olds with my mother's flannel graph. On my last visit to my parents' house, my mother asked if I would like to take her entire Bible set of flannel graphs. She thinks her days of teaching children have passed, since her current focus seems to be in women's ministry. Humbly, I accepted her offer. Now one of my mother's prized resources for teaching Bible stories has been passed to my children. On Sundays when we use these beautiful pictures, our normally wiggly three-year-olds sit quietly at her feet. Listening intently, they inch closer as her story continues. As I watched her on that Sunday, I grabbed my phone and snapped a picture. Then I smiled contentedly. In a few moments, my mother had received a text with that picture and the word *heritage*. She agreed.

My middle child excels in almost everything she tries. While she would shy away from this compliment, it is true. With music, academics, speech, debate, and sports, she has success. Nothing thrills me more than watching her teach children, use puppets, or lead worship. All the small steps of training seem to be coming together. My heart is glad.

The boys find numerous ways to serve in children's work, running the sound board; serving food at functions; helping out at Salvation Army fundraisers, POW luncheons, and work days; and so much more. A life of service is a rich, fulfilling life. My husband and I work to set the example of serving in organized, regular ways as well as in sudden, unexpected daily gestures when a need presents itself. These patterns are passed down from parents on both sides with examples of generosity to mimic.

Joseph serving at the POW Appreciation Lunch at the Peabody Hotel

As we began our parenting journey some twenty years ago, I knew without hesitation that I wanted to school my children at home. One of the not-so-great things about being a missionary kid is that you are moved from place to place and school to school. From kindergarten through third grade, I was home-schooled in the West Indies. In those years, nobody used the term *homeschooling*. My mother had the option of sending us to a boarding school or keeping us at home for school. The island that we lived on lacked schools of any kind. Even though my mother was young, she was vehemently opposed to a boarding school for her children. I am really grateful that she chose to keep us with her. Those years of school seem pleasant and peaceful in my memories.

Homeschooling in St. Lucia with Starla

Homeschooling in St. Lucia with Mom

As I was approaching fourth grade, my family returned to the United States for a one-year furlough. It was during these early years in a traditional school setting that I discovered I was an ugly duckling. Although on the outside I looked like those of the children in my school, on the inside I had never lived in the United States. I did not know the games and clothes. All culture around me was foreign. Academics were dull in large groups; I have often felt that way about traditional school. Large groups usually require that you wait for those who need the material repeated or for those who were not listening the first time or the tenth time. Teachers cannot allow for discussion in such a sizable crowd. Most tragically, the playground in this setting was supervised by the students themselves. So the bully ran the games, none of which I had ever heard of. This ensured that I would be chosen last every single day. While many factors contributed to the emotional distress I felt during that time, I longed for the days of schooling at home.

Sixth grade dropped me into a completely new culture in which I was ostracized for my white skin. That exclusion, combined with complete academic boredom in public school, had me longing again for the days of schooling at home. Seventh grade involved a three-hour bus ride to a private school in another city. Halfway through seventh grade, I begged my mom to allow me to work at home on my school assignments. She relented. Efficient as a student, I finished my seventh-grade year home-schooling. When I was in eighth grade, we moved again where I attended a nearby public school. Public school proved academically boring, physically threatening, and socially intimidating. One significant happy experience was participating in a ukulele band as the sole guitar player. While I was eager to make friends, the boys seemed to be on a testosterone roller coaster, and the girls were involved in numerous dramas. The best thing about my eighth-grade year was meeting Shari Todd, one of my favorite people even to this day. Later, in high school, we added Susan Kaneshiro, who completed our trio. She is also one of my favorite people. We still love to spend time together.

Vance Family circa 1984

High school was a jumble of some homeschooling and then private school. Those four years involved four different school experiences. Not a great way to establish memories with one group of people. Such uprooting is common for missionary and military kids. So, when reviewing my personal experiences, schooling at home won out as my favorite experience. I could work at my own speed with time to pursue my own interests when school was completed. Don't misunderstand my skills. I am just an average brain who is a hard worker with a standard of excellence.

When schooling at home, I aimed to complete what I deemed boring or hard subjects early in the day or early in the week.

When I was finished, my time was my own to pursue reading, playing my guitar, and photography. In the spirit of homeschooling, my mother encouraged to me to take some outside instruction in my senior year of high school. I took an adult typing class and enrolled in a genuine photography school. Back in the days of film, students completed photography assignments with time in the darkroom to develop their film. What fun! To this day, I remember the skills I learned as I worked through those assignments with a professional photographer.

College offered consistency for four years. My years as a student taught me to devour learning. Homeschooling is not the path for everyone, but it was my favorite experience. From the time my children were young, reading took a significant portion of our day. Books offer tantalizing adventures and conversations with people here and gone, and they plant a myriad of ideas in our imaginations. Reading a book together is like going on an adventure together.

I wrote much of this book hidden away for a few days while my children were at camp. Quiet times of reflection remind me of my days as a teenager. Those years in Hawaii were lonely, because no one my age seemed intent on pursuing a relationship with God. I often stayed home when friends were going out, because I did not want to participate in the activities they had planned. One evening when I assumed that we were headed out for a time of just hanging out together, I had found myself in dangerous and illegal situation. After that, I opted out of evening time with friends. Once work and school were completed, I spent my free time reading my Bible, praying, and playing the guitar. Those hours of quiet with the Lord established a deep trust and my relationship with him.

I always wanted to be a mom who would mimic what my mother had done for me. You have heard it said that we learn more from what our parents *do* than from what they *say*. This is true. In my own adult life, I am trying to do more than I say.

When I was a young girl growing up in the West Indies, my mother would rise early to read and pray on the back patio. Although I knew I was not to interrupt her, this daily exercise created curiosity in me. Regularly, I overheard her praying out loud. Her relationship with God seemed as real and genuine as her relationship with me or anyone else she could touch and see. I wanted to know him too. So I began to read my Bible, memorize Scriptures, and journal about the truth I was learning. I prayed for needs and developed thanksgiving in my heart while conversing with God throughout my day.

It wasn't until I was in my late thirties that I discovered how special it was to have the discipline of constant prayer and talk with God. Several long-term and seemingly committed Christians expressed that they had never really heard God speaking to them in the middle of an ordinary day. I had believed that most mature Christians easily carried on that constant back-and-forth talk with Him. Sadly, most of those I asked said they would like to be so intimate, but their communication with God was not as clearly detectible. I was stunned. I was sad. I was sobered. My God had been my constant companion in conversation since I was a little girl. How deeply grateful I am that this has been my journey! He calls each of us into that intimate place in which we can do life with him. "Draw near to God, and he will draw near to you...." He promises in James 4:8a ESV. Pursuing God creates a center for all that life can possibly throw at you.

Although my dad was shy about his role in our lives directly, he studied diligently to bring a fresh message to the pulpit on Sundays. He emphasized reading the word of God individually. His appreciation for the local people we reached on the mission field developed many of them into fine scholars of God's Word.

He loved my mom and each of us well. His library was full of the most wonderful books. When I was a teenager, I loved to borrow books from his shelves. Both of my parents are active readers, so it follows that I love books immensely too.

Dad invested in his children with lots of hugs and encouragement. While our family did not have much financially, we had a rich family life. We now have twenty-six extended family members, and our heritage is rich with Godly direction and love of family.

My extended family consists of two brothers and one sister and their families. My siblings have remained close knit as we do life together, work through illnesses, raising kids, job changes and just growing in new ways. I am thankful for Nathan and Shannon, Daphne and Rob along with Titus and Diane. All of us are married once with healthy relationships. We do a yearly vacation together so that we can spend more time making memories and catching up. This is not a small blessing. I am grateful. I am proud of each of them.

As a mom, I am stretched every day by life to pursue Him and respond in a holy way. I fail many times every day. But God knows my heart. His Word offers wisdom and clear direction. Some may feel that only certain people are chosen to have a special relationship with God. Know that he loves everyone. He loves *you*! John 3:16 verifies for us that "God so loved the world that He gave His only son that whosoever believes in Him should not perish, but have everlasting life." I believe He invites us all. If this is not your reality, pursue Him. This journey will help you be the best mother you could ever be. Your reason for doing everything revolves around the outpouring of your love for God in response to His love for you. Just writing that gives me chills. Don't miss this joy. If you are already a child of God, don't miss the joy of living in fellowship with Him daily.

This idea of God's tangible presence was further verified by a conversation I had several years ago. A new friend shared that she had been brought up in an ungodly home in which a series of nightmares was her reality every day and every night. In this darkness, she clung to God. She spoke to Him regularly, long before anyone had introduced her to church or the Bible. God was reality to that child grasping for the security and love of her Heavenly Father.

Missionary stories about isolated people and groups who already know the story of God's great love and redemption verify what Romans 2 tells us: that "those who do not have the word of God by nature understand and do the word of God...They show that the word of law is written on their hearts while their conscience also bears witness." God is calling us to an intimate relationship with Him. Why miss out? Seize hold of His hand.

If you grasp only one concept in this book, I hope it is the idea of drawing close to God. Developing spiritual disciplines of prayer and reading the Scripture should be at the forefront of your efforts every day. This would be the best path for being a better wife, mother, and homeschooler. On my journey, I have certainly felt dry and empty patches. We all do. Our hearts long for the filling of God. The more familiar we are with the Scripture, the more wisdom comes to us as we mother and school our little ones. This inner strength grows us as women who love our men better too. Our confidence is in who God made us, not in the changing materialism of the world around us.

A myriad of discussions with moms desperate to ask questions about homeschooling launched the idea for this book. Whether they were new moms entering homeschooling for the first time or current homeschoolers with young children quickly entering a new level of school, they posed many of the same questions. Even my husband began to recognize the repetition of questions. For these moms, of course, the questions needed urgent answers. I remember having many of the same pressing questions. Through reading, asking more experienced moms, and praying for wisdom and direction, I found my way. Eagerly and patiently, I found myself responding to the same concerns. My husband suggested a book. I laughed. These ideas and answers seemed so familiar to me now because I had sought answers diligently. But for others just stepping onto the path, I hope these ideas offer a helping hand. Certainly, these are just the ideas compiled from my journey. As I am raising my children, the wisdom extended by those ahead and the truth of the Bible are what shed logic in the daily trenches.

CHAPTER 1

Getting Started

First, determine your goals for homeschooling. Some parents select homeschooling because they are running from something. A teacher who does not understand his learning style may discourage their student. The school environment may not be strict enough to force the child's behavior into compliance. Bullies may be threatening their student, creating a fearful setting that prevents any cognitive progress. Others choose homeschooling because they cannot imagine their child spending all day away from them. They enjoy the joys and challenges of parenting. Some desire a private-school education for their child but cannot afford it. Homeschooling seems a viable route to reach this level of education. Still others dream of what their entire child could be if they custom design her education and skill-building development.

Support of Spouse

Whatever situation brings a parent to educate at home, a supportive spouse combined with assessment of both the parent and child makes for the strong foundation necessary to plan the student's education experience. Often the dad proposes homeschooling for the children. Frequently, one parent is more eager and ready for the commitments involved in the lifestyle of homeschooling. Educating oneself about the time, cost, and lifestyle of homeschooling creates a more successful adventure. As I mentioned in the introduction, my decision originated from more empirical reasoning.

Investigate the cost of schooling at home compared to the cost of private or public options. Even children enrolled in public school incur costs. The public school may require uniforms and fees for sports or band. It will take time to determine the cost of homeschooling your student. Each family has different goals. Each child needs an individual plan. This cost varies greatly, based on the number of children in the family, supplies available from previous years, used resources that can be bought or borrowed, and decisions on curriculum. Spend the time and energy necessary to secure the support of the reluctant spouse. To feel confident, some may need more information or to meet some successful homeschoolers. Take the time to tackle the reluctant parent's concerns. It is worth the investment. A team approach proves invaluable.

Assessing Parents' Strengths and Weaknesses

Each parent considering the seriousness of being responsible for his or her child's education must pause to consider his or her own strengths and weaknesses. Perhaps these are known easily. Write them down. Ask your mother, sister, close friends, or your spouse to respond to your list. Perhaps they will deny or embellish your evaluation of these qualities. Let's say that you love to read. This feature promises that you will more willingly trudge through the book catalogs, used-book sales, and lesson preparation.

If you enjoyed your years as a young student, schooling might present an unexpected opportunity to relearn and absorb subjects. If you were not an eager student, now may be the time to find the excitement of acquiring knowledge with your child. Just watching a child progress is sheer excitement. Whether or not you maximized your own educational experiences, your child deserves to benefit from ongoing excitement concerning his education.

Other strengths that add to the ease of schooling include organization, attention to detail, a playful spirit, relational strengths, and a servant attitude, just to name a few. From one perspective, a naturally organized mom will look ahead to the long-term goals for her student's educational experience as well as at the month and year ahead. Equally valuable is the ability to make learning fun. After establishing goals and ordering them into hourly segments or daily assignments, a parent must douse her plan with grace. Consistently expecting the unexpected each day will allow her to adjust accordingly. Working toward a goal always produces a more productive result. When a student does not complete a list, one can still celebrate all that she has accomplished. Approaching every day with just a vague idea of what must be done certainly finds much less accomplished. Long-term goals are much more difficult to achieve without strategizing how to meet them bit by bit.

A playful spirit stimulates ideas and learning games, which lull students into learning while diverting them from the necessary rigors of school. For example, plugging away through workbook pages in language followed by a bingo word game stimulates academic progress while adding in the fun factor. Memorizing geography by constructing a puzzle proves entirely more enjoyable than simply working out of a book. An extensive world of educational games and manipulatives exists. Locate inspiring accessories through catalogs, the local school store, and the Internet. Your student may accomplish sizable jumps in knowledge just by playing.

Develop positive relational skills that encourage the student to learn to interact properly with others of all ages. If a parent possesses tact, discernment, and manners, her student will absorb even more if they spend more time together homeschooling. A child attending school in a traditional setting misses so much of his mother's interaction with others on a daily basis. Making the most of growing up together is one of the best perks of homeschooling.

Practicing a servant attitude with your child benefits the student greatly. A do-as-I-do approach can be easily mimicked. When a family determines its own schedule, intentional planning to serve may locate more opportunities. Since homeschooling allows the student to work ahead or make up work on the weekend, a full day of serving is feasible. Giving to others provides insight into what a student should be grateful for in her opportunities and gifts.

Weaknesses that affect homeschooling may include disorganization, poor time management, unattainable expectations, and irritability, all of which may be adjusted with prayer and proper training. Numerous resources exist to improve organization. My book offers many ideas. Poor time management appears to be a combination of lack of willpower and intentionality. If you want something badly enough, you usually do what is necessary to get it. Therefore, if you desire your student to succeed academically, school will start at the designated 8:00 a.m. or soon after 8:00 a.m. Schoolbooks will be completed each year. Housework will be accomplished as a team. When all seems overwhelming or hopeless, it is helpful just to put one foot in front of the other.

Some dream with expectations too large. (I am raising my hand in confession.) The challenge, then, becomes selecting the best and eliminating the good. A conscientious effort toward achievable goals enhanced by some dreaming works beautifully!

Determine it. Pray it. Accomplish it.

Assessing Your Child's Strengths and Weaknesses

Effective planning involves assessment by both observing behavior and evaluating written testing. As a parent, you likely observe your child's strengths and weaknesses in academics and in other areas such as church and serving opportunities. Your strongest qualities are likely your greatest weaknesses. Knowing this is both encouraging and disheartening. Annual testing aids the knowledge of my students' academic standing as well. Let me mention here that looking through testing results requires pensive effort. For example, say your student scores poorly in grammar. Noticing that the student missed only seven of the twenty questions that make up this part of the test may bring more clarity. Perhaps a yearly or biannual extensive evaluation best benefits both student and parent.

This section outlines how I look at my kids twice a year to see if all is tracking along with God's best for our children. Ted Tripp's *Shepherding Your Child's Heart*, which I read once a year as a refresher, inspired some of these ideas. Before I had kids, I diligently used my Franklin Covey planner to assess myself in a variety of areas such as these. When I became a mom, I thought that looking through to the big picture frequently might aid me in doing the day-to-day tasks more meaningfully.

Locate a place for intentional planning for your student. This brainstorming stays in my planner behind one of my tabs. Each page goes something like this:

Joseph: Elementary Student, Age Ten, Entering Fifth Grade

Academics

Bible—AWANA

English—Language 6 (Abeka), Spelling 6 (Abeka)
Institute for Excellence in Writing (IEW) writing class using the theme-based books for three years (fourth grade through seventh grade)
Literature books from Sonlight and Veritas Press

Math—Math 5 (Abeka), Abeka, assorted math games, speed drills

History—Reading book one of *Mystery of History*, audiobooks, books from Sonlight and Veritas Press catalogs. (Remember that he is child number five, so he has a large collection of resources to select from in our family library.)

Science—Zoology II (Apologia) and anatomy along with a wide variety of other science books. One of our favorites this month is the Usborne Science Encyclopedia. Remember, this child loves to read!

Music—Piano lessons

Spiritual Development

Writing Bible verses in personal journal in the morning

Family Bible time

AWANA

AWANA Bible quiz competition in February

Apologetics for NCFCA

Service opportunities (helping sister teach three-year-olds, car care for widows and elderly at church)

Physical Development

Recreational sports—Basketball, baseball, soccer

Golf with Dad

Social Development

Learning to cook

Eating smart—Selecting foods that nourish

Friend time

Mikayla: High-School Student, Age Fourteen, Entering Ninth Grade

Academics

English—Literature, grammar, vocabulary/spelling

Math—Geometry

Science—Marine biology

History—World history (Omnibus II & world geography notebook)

Language—Latin II

Speech/debate

Music—Flute and piano

Spiritual Development

Personal devotions

Family time on prayer and names of God

Sunday's activities and times for serving others

Apologetics

Service opportunities—AWANA or preschool Sunday-school class

Mission trip

Physical Development

Soccer (fall)

Discussing nutrients, diet

Growth spurt currently

New pediatrician

Swimming—Water safety instructor (WSI)

Social Development

Driver's permit in December

New, sharp friends

Contributions around the house, such as learning to clean and maintain family space, cars, and personal space (bedroom)

Test Review

Reviewing written tests might necessitate a change in schedule more than anything. For example, say your student struggles with spelling. His scores show you what you already know on this subject. Perhaps the morning should begin with spelling. Instead of just doing what has been done in spelling, add another process. In most schedules, math, Bible, spelling, memorized material, and music should be done first in the day. Celebrate with a protein snack once you have worked hard on these energy-demanding skills.

If your student is deemed behind in math, start doing mental math on car trips. Abeka has a fun set of mental math cards. We call out a series of numbers with their processes and wait for the first correct answer. For example, $12 + 17 = 29 - 6 = 23 + 72 = 95 - 20 = 75$. So, the final answer is 75. Think of how practicing this sort of math is helpful as a shopper. Practice giving a price and asking your child how certain discounted percentages change the price. (See chapter 11 for more ideas, such as bingo games and oral word problems.)

As you write down each area of your child's development, pray. Ask God to show you what He intends for this season of growth. Seek solutions to areas of need. Pray for your child's friends. Pray for the new places she will go in the new semester. Evaluate where changes can be made. Celebrate progress! These times of reflection give confidence that aimlessness is not behind the next step. Purposeful thought and movement always produce the best result. Ask God to help you visualize the needs of your child in the next growth period. Sit quietly and pray for each child's needs.

Support Moms—Networking

Participating in a community with other like-minded moms may prove to be just as much a part of your success as a homeschooler as selecting the right curriculum for your student. If such a group does not exist in your area, building a cluster of such moms will be worth all your effort.

Groups may be centered around field trips, a book club, or skill sharing. Determine your needs. Look for a current group. Be active in securing like-minded girlfriends. If you are a new mom, a group with moms who are just beginning as well as moms who are experienced might be just right for you. Some moms gravitate toward larger groups while others prefer a smaller mix.

Look for moms who share your learning goals. For example, if you strive toward excellence, don't settle into a group of unschoolers. This term can be defined in numerous ways, but most agree that this pattern of schooling involves leaving the child to explore subjects that interest him. For the very rare self-motivated child, this might result in excellence. But for too many children, this plan would result in laziness and nonproductively. Imagine if a student was left to do math or vocabulary only if it seemed interesting. So many parts of education require structure for success.

If your family leans toward structured days, you might benefit from others who know how best to order a successful schedule. Much of what I look for in a gathering of ladies is their heart for the Lord. As they love the Lord intensely, they love their families with the same fervor. Many of the other particulars fall into place once this central common feature is determined.

Establishing a support network with moms who communicate in a godly manner is essential. Positive conversation and confidentiality, as well as loyalty, greatly contribute to healthy friendships. A pattern of not gossiping, a determination to build one another up, and discussions that honor God make for a healthy mom's group. To speak of these as goals at the beginning of each semester is a healthy review. Spending time speaking well of one another in a group environment raises morale too.

Look for fellow moms in your church family. A class your student takes may offer a meeting of like-minded moms. Consider a book club. Perhaps your mom friends would enjoy reading a selected book each month. If you meet every first Thursday, for example, you might discuss the book over shared snacks. Or you could just meet and talk about your favorite reading from the previous month. An experienced mom could speak on a special topic at each meeting.

Another idea is to share skills. For example, if one mom is known for her bread making, she could host a demonstration. Another meeting might highlight a mom who is an expert on searching for scholarships. Still another mom might share about the ministry that her family serves in weekly. The ideas for such get-togethers are unlimited. Investigate your needs and the needs of your friends. Take turns planning the get-togethers. Make the gatherings meet the needs and interests of the group.

Other Ideas for Moms' Meetings

Freezer cooking. Invite five moms to participate. Each mom brings five nine-by-thirteen-inch pans of her assigned main dish ready to freeze, along with one eight-by-eight-inch pan to share that evening as a sample. Dishes are selected together with criteria such as a specific weight for the meat in each pan. Some churches do bulk cooking for fund-raising events. Many recipes exist for successful cooking.

Book club. Assigned books or topics for each month develop a fascinating roundtable discussion.

Special speakers. Moms in the group take turns hosting a night with a special speaker. Each mom could bring three dollars to put in a thank-you note as a gift for the speaker.

Theme nights. Picking a theme such as cooking, decorating, food gifts, or organization sparks attendance and excitement. A questionnaire at the beginning of planning for this will guarantee that specific needs and desires are met when the themes are selected.

Determining the Requirements

Once homeschooling is the selected route for your child's education, investigate your state's requirements. Read about the requirements for any colleges and universities that might be in your child's future. Although this last idea may seem extreme, look closely at what is ahead. Many academic charts ask you to determine whether your child just wants to graduate from high school or plans to attend college. Some students might pursue a two-year degree or skill training instead of college after high school.

For a college-bound student, I suggest the following:

Math—4 years (Algebra I, Geometry, Algebra II, Precalculus, or Trigonometry)

English—4 years (English I, II, III, IV, Writing, Literature, Grammar, and Vocabulary)

Science—3–4 years with labs (Biology I, Biology II, Anatomy, Physics, Chemistry)

History—3 years (US History, World History, and Geography). Our students do the Veritas Omnibus program as a core of our history requirements.

Personal finance—0.5 year

PE/wellness/nutrition—1.5 years

Electives—6–8 years

Language—2 years

Fine arts—1 year (speech, debate, music lessons, band, or music history)

Many students select photography, computer-related classes, video editing, auto mechanics, band, driver's education, or home economics as electives.

Discussing the Big Picture

Most successful people agree that each child is multifaceted. As you approach the challenging and hard work of each day, think ahead to your goals. Keep the finish line in the forefront of your mind when you are tired, when your desk is calling, when the house needs deep cleaning, when you yearn for lunch with a friend, when you would love to attend a morning Bible study, when you can't seem to master that math lesson, or when myriad other desires pull you away from the task of schooling your child. Although you should not lose yourself, and you should schedule time for refueling, don't forget your vision.

Dream the future. Commit to today. Love your child.

CHAPTER 2

Education and Learning Styles

> I think this is the most extraordinary
> collection of talent, of human knowledge,
> that has ever been gathered together at
> the White House, with the exception of
> when Thomas Jefferson dined alone.
> —PRESIDENT JOHN F. KENNEDY, DURING A
> DINNER HONORING NOBEL PRIZE WINNERS

What astounds us about Thomas Jefferson? Is it his innovative, self-conceived portable desk that held the precious documents of our infant country? Is it the massive, extensively cataloged library that he graciously gifted his beloved country when her library burned at the hands of enemies? Is it his passion and appealing gift for words that shaped the language of our own Declaration of Independence? Is it his love for limited government that reduced national debt by one-third during his presidency?

For me, all these things identify a man who deeply loved learning. His ardor to master so wide a range of subjects speaks to his insatiable desire to discover as many mysteries of God's world as his life span allowed. God created us to worship Him. In unearthing the depth of any subject, man confronts His greatness. Recently, a mom new to homeschooling told me that her family left traditional school to *learn*. Her boys soon engaged aggressively in science, Socratic circle discussions, and intensive reading. Although the days proved challenging, nothing their family had ever experienced prior to homeschooling approached being as educationally satisfying.

Traditional Public or Private

The traditional style of education most popularly includes public and secular private schools. Public-school students account for about 90 percent of school attendance in the United States in 2017. Just fewer than 10 percent of American students are considered enrollees in the private options.[1]

Many parents select public education because it is free or because it is what everyone else is doing. Others assess that they are paying taxes for the public schools, so they might as well get their money's worth. A significant number of others were educated in the public-school system. They felt that it worked for them, so it will work for their children. Some parents don't concern themselves with the details surrounding their child's education. They feel comfortable leaving the development of their child to others.

Maybe this is because they feel that others are more expert on the subject. Perhaps they are too busy to do the work of finding out what their child needs and creating an environment that is parent directed. Every parent has reasons for selecting the particular educational path of each of their children.

Private secular schools are most often gender specific, military, or based on a religious preference. The cost of these options varies significantly based on numerous factors. Most encourage greater input from parents and offer more extracurricular activities and additional scholarship paths for graduates. Some of the best public schools offer these advantages, but most public schools do not offer the same advantages as a private option. Each school offers unique benefits. Parents need to ask lots of questions and use their best research skills.

Christian schools are listed under traditional private schools. A Christian education is always more expensive to the parents in dollars than is a public education. Obviously, this is because public schools are funded by tax dollars while those selecting private education pay taxes that fund the public schools and pay for private education. A popular idea is tax credits for those who choose an educational option other than that of the public schools. The truth is that even senior adults who will never benefit from the public schools in their area contribute financially with their tax dollars. Sometimes a Christian school offers a safer student environment. Other times, a school is so desperate for additional students that it takes rejects from other schools. This usually creates chaos. In the best of situations, a Christian school combines high-quality education with Biblical instruction, enriching clubs, and sports. Ideally, daily training and experiences give students a rich spiritual background.

Models of Education

One of the key decisions in homeschooling is selecting a learning method. If you tackle this with the aim of excellence, you must read a great deal and ask an abundance of questions. In this chapter, you will find some of the most popular thoughts behind homeschooling. Not surprisingly, school techniques vary from school to school even in traditional settings. Each family, mother, and student represents unique likes and dislikes. Each person boasts favorite subjects and interests.

Cynthia Tobias's *The Way We Learn* provides a host of options to motivate and stimulate academic illumination. How delightful that being homeschooled means your education can be personalized! These descriptions represent just a brief explanation; you can explore each of these learning styles in numerous books. One great advantage of home education is the mixing of the styles with various students or with subjects. For example, our home incorporates traditional learning for math, spelling, and grammar. In history and science, we mix the unit studies with classical, literature-rich pursuits.

Unschooling

John Holt popularized this approach in the 1940s. Proponents believe that a child-led approach maximizes learning. Advocates state that most learning occurs naturally throughout the course of events during the day. Planning upsets the natural flow of learning. Some promote delayed learning, especially for boys, who tend to be more active. This method might work well for self-motivated, self-propelled individuals who enjoy pacing themselves, but others, left alone without a schedule, might waste time. The eclectic style of unschooling lends itself to some exciting field trips and long rabbit chases through resource material when acted out with prudence.

Unit studies

Unit studies are some of the most exciting adventures you will ever have as a family. They can be incorporated into a school year or used as summer fun. You don't have to be a homeschooler to create unit studies. The best moms always generate fun! Secretly, you must know that tucking these into your vacation allows you to accomplish "school" under the guise of "summer." All the while you are freeing up your school year by doing some intensive activity in the more leisurely months.

When used during the school year, a unit study may accompany math and grammar to complete the needed studies. Unit studies easily combine science and history.

When I first started homeschooling, I met one of my all-time favorite people, Katherine Barnhart. She loved being a mom, loved homeschooling, loved doing school on a large picnic table under the trees, loved field trips, and loved baking large quantities of bread for her family and others. One of her treasured activities was KONOS. Michael Farris, president of the Home School Legal Defense Association (HSLDA), names this program "the granddaddy of unit studies," because it was the original. Simply put, students study history or science by going deep and expanding to include many subjects. Parents of traditionally schooled children would immensely enjoy this activity as well. Unit studies can be purchased already created, planned, and compiled, or you can build one on your own.

Let me give you two examples. Let's say you want to study botany with your elementary-aged kids. My favorite primary source would be Apologia's *Botany*. Add products to do the experiments. Select a journal for notebooking or purchase the one they offer. Add drawings. Record walks. Make notes. Personalize the notebook by creating a unique cover that expresses the student. Add pressed flowers. Add pencil drawings. Add discovery photos. The ideas are endless. The student has practiced art, photography, reading, observation, note taking, dictation, flower pressing, the history of plants, the history of related locations, and on and on. Imagination knows no limits. Truly, this is comparable to being on a fabulous vacation together. Think of the treasure this book will become in years ahead.

Next, consider a geography notebook. This summer we will begin on a geography notebook for all our children. My family *loves* maps! This obsession was inherited from their mother. A six-foot-by-eight-foot world map from the National Geographic Society engulfs one wall in our schoolroom. Over the years, we have memorized hundreds of countries, capital cities, geographic locations, physical features, and other facts. I have a dream. Seriously, I have been thinking of this idea for more than five years. We will start with a section on the physical geography of the world. Next, we will embark on a lengthy tour of each continent. Each child will decorate a notebook suited to his or her liking. Although creating a personalized cover seems like a small detail to complete in the beginning of this geography notebook, consider that this initial activity marries the idea to the child's heart. Or so I hope.

This geography notebook will likely take about two years to complete. My resources are piled into a bookshelf in our schoolroom. Puzzles, books, maps, and such are waiting. Each continent section includes the exploration of physical features, countries, history, and cultural studies along with the history of how God has moved in these places.

Sometimes my children tire of my enthusiasm toward learning. One day, I hope they will all join me enthusiastically in this pursuit of knowledge. Happily, my girls are extremely enthusiastic about our Omnibus and etymology for the fall. (They did resist the urge to look at our etymology textbooks when they arrived in May, but that might be asking too much.) Any type of adventure will reveal the wonder of details given to us by our loving God. Such activities offer me one of the best perks of being a homeschool mom: delving into something that I missed as a student myself.

Look up the numerous sources that offer suggestions and options for notebooking or unit studies.

Charlotte Mason

Charlotte Mason was a British educator who lived in the late 1800s and early 1900s. Her method, the Charlotte Mason method, is centered on the idea that education is three pronged: education is an atmosphere, a discipline, and a life.

By *atmosphere*, Charlotte meant the surroundings in which the child grows up. A child absorbs a lot from his home environment. Charlotte believed that atmosphere makes up one-third of a child's education.

By *discipline*, Charlotte meant the discipline of good habits—specifically, habits of character. Cultivating good habits in your child's life makes up another third of his education.

The other third of education, *life*, applies to academics. Charlotte believed that we should give children living thoughts and ideas, not just dry facts. So, all her methods for teaching the various school subjects are built around that concept.

For example, Charlotte's students used living books rather than dry textbooks. Living books are usually written in story form by one author who has a passion for the subject. A living book makes the subject come alive.

She taught spelling by using passages from great books that communicate great ideas rather than from just a list of words.

She encouraged spending time outdoors, interacting with God's creation firsthand, and learning the living ways of nature.

Some of the most popular learning activities that implement this style are the lap books and the nature journals. Numerous sources explain these two ideas. Both concepts ramp up the fun in learning while creating a beautiful keepsake. It is like making a journal or scrapbook for the layers of learning in a selected subject. History, science, and geography lend themselves easily to these concepts.[2]

Classical

The classical schooling of today comes partially from Dorothy Sayres's *Lost Tools of Learning*, Susan Bauer Wise's *The Well-Trained Mind*, and Charlotte Mason's ideas. Numerous resources and curricula are available to blend these thoughts. Highlighted in these books is the love of learning through both books and hands-on experience. Taking notes on learning experiences and communicating through writing and speaking ensure the student a unique learning environment.

Literature-rich classical schooling best describes our family's pattern. Classical education differs from other types by highlighting the significant reading of great books throughout all the years of school. Other characteristics involve the study of Greek and Latin roots along with a heavy emphasis on the three stages of learning. Some who love the Charlotte Mason approach blend it with the classical approach. As in other areas of life, one can love many different things and select what he or she deems best in each.

Latin is not critical for classical education, but it is highly beneficial when added intermittently or consistently. For challenged learners, it can be incorporated into vocabulary and spelling studies or omitted to focus on just the core academics. Although its value is immeasurable, the study of Latin or Greek is an option. Realistically, some struggling learners need to focus on the core subjects requiring memorization. For those who can absorb all subjects, the benefit of learning Latin is the ability to absorb any of the Romance languages, such as Spanish, French, and Portuguese. Latin is the source of nearly 75 to 80 percent of all words in these languages.[3]

Western civilization as we know it today has Greek and Latin origins. The advantages of a student who emerges from an education rich in Latin study are numerous. His grasp of English grammar improves. With a Latin base, he can more easily seize all subjects. Most agree that those who study Latin tend to be more purists when communicating in English. Since these students assimilate more words as well as interpreting those that are unfamiliar, they score higher on standardized tests. From my personal experience, our Latin pursuit enhances English grammar, Spanish, all sciences, etymology, and writing.

Music naturally interests most people who delight in classical studies. Music education benefits all students, regardless of their retention or lifelong ability to play the practiced instrument. Just working through the skill of reading music coordinated with placing your hands and feet correctly on the selected instrument demands concentration and skill. Equally challenging is true adeptness at summoning and mastering the gift of voice, whether used solo or synchronized with others. For all those reasons and more, music is frequently married to the pursuit of academic knowledge.

Finally in this brief assessment of classical quests, the progress of education seems properly placed in the three stages of learning: grammar, dialectic, and rhetoric. Grammar begins as early as the development in the womb, such as how a mother feels toward her child, how she might sing, and the music or reading the child hears. It continues with a slew of early-learned facts such as the grammar of spiritual truths absorbed through Bible memory. The linguistics of numerous subjects requires attention. If a student assimilates them in the early years, when she is between ten and twelve years old, they remain in recall to speed up further mastery. How lovely to approach a seemingly new subject only to find that you are well acquainted with the grammar of so much of it! You can skip to the understanding of it.

The dialectic stage is easily perceived, as it is marked by a series of questions. Discussion, debate, reasoning, logic, and deliberation married to a healthy environment promise a positive outcome. This process is the making of a boy or girl into a man or woman.

Not to be forgotten is the rhetoric stage, which promises to be the icing on the cake. Only by communicating through writing and speaking can the earlier training reach full maturity. Although refinement in this way can be awkward, practice and experience bring great fulfillment.

Classical Christian with Literature-Rich Classical Education

Thomas Jefferson ranks as one of my favorite Americans, as you might have guessed from comments at the beginning of this chapter. At first glance, it might seem that my enthusiasm stems from his insatiable appetite for learning and his immense collection of books. While both of these features warm my heart toward this patriot, I glean the most from his thoughts on education. As a proponent of classical education, he stated, "For classical learning I have ever been a zealous advocate." He claimed, "I cannot live without books," which is the case for me also. A true confession would reveal that I have called our home insurance provider to ensure that our policy is sufficient to cover the mass of books we keep in our home.

Some time ago, during a visit with a most hospitable family, I felt something was odd. After consideration of the cause, I concluded that this home completely lacked books. Sadly, media filled their place. Many homes never enjoy the delicious adventures of a book read out loud. If backed into a corner, I would say that my favorite moments of schooling my children at home come from reading books together. Along with an extensive assignment of personal reading, our style is a literature-rich classical education.

> Thomas Jefferson amassed literally thousands of books in his library at Monticello. When the nation's library burned during the War of 1812, British forces had entered Washington, DC, burning the Capitol building and three-thousand-volume library inside it. Jefferson expressed his particular distress at this loss: "I learn from the newspapers that the vandalism of our enemy has triumphed at Washington over science as well as the arts, by the destruction of the public library with the noble edifice in which it was deposited."[4]

Recognizing that it would be difficult for Congress to re-place the library that had been lost, given the war and the difficulty of procuring items from Europe, Thomas Jefferson offered up his large personal library to Congress after the British burned the Library of Congress during the War of 1812. Jefferson, utterly distraught by this news, sought to offer his personal collection to his beloved country. He knew that funds were not available to replace the valuable collec-tion that had existed, and he had already intended to will his collection to the library, so it seemed fitting to offer it when the need proved urgent. His carefully selected collection of 6,707 books traveled to the nation's capital in the original bookshelves. In mid-April of 1815, the books journeyed in ten wagons to Washington, arriving in mid-May.[5]

For a literature-rich learning environment, choose classic books over textbooks. Many sources have profitable reading lists for all age groups. Some of my favorite sources are Veritas Press, Sonlight, and our local classical school. Search for books from these sources, used-book sales, eBay, and Amazon. Ask fellow homeschoolers where they find the best deals.

As a lover of the spiritual ideal embodied in a vast array of people from the past as well as today, I find biographies and historical fiction irreplaceable inspirations for our children. Combining stories of Biblical people, people from history, and today's giants motivates all of us to a more purposeful, impactful life. All of us are inspired when we hear of hardships overcome, of an under-dog who wins, of a life well finished, or of a seemingly "regular" person achieving significantly. Fleshing out the hard things in life as we walk in another's shoes motivates us to press toward necessary changes in our own lives. Seeing the failures and successes of ordinary people stirs in a child the grit to do more, to do better, and to do right.

A literature-rich education cannot be overvalued.

Stories excite! Read more! Live more!

Eclectic

The eclectic mom selects what she likes best from a variety of sources and then combines them to meet her style.

We are blessed with so many resources and options. Let me give you an example of how the collected plays out in my home. I have always selected Abeka resources for our math and language studies. Most years we have also used a backup for spelling and grammar. As I discuss further in this book, we combine traditional resources with unit studies, field trips, notebooking, and assigned reading books when studying history.

Science in my home combines traditional resources with notebooking. In science, we lean toward selecting one topic per semester. This year, my younger boys, who are rising sixth and seventh graders, will complete general science and then delve into a physics and chemistry book geared toward junior-high students. Sometime in the spring, they will attend a three-day lab intensive complementing their general-science studies. For us, general science is an easy review. We also studied chemistry and physics for a semester about two years ago.

Elementary science lessons for my children have included intensive study on botany, astronomy, physics, chemistry, weather, birds, water creatures, land animals, and more. Science is a combination of book study, rabbit chases online, notebooking, and field trips. (Rabbit chases are intense searches for more information on a subject that interests the student.) High-school years follow a more traditional path in science.

But we study science in every venue possible. Science museums, aquariums, estuaries, pioneer days, botanical gardens, IMAX films, conversations with science-minded people, selected science-intensive labs at the zoo, and an eye out for nature all contribute to celebrating and understanding God's creation. Since my family members are all photographers, we use our camera lenses as microscopes and viewfinders to discover the intricacies of life around us. As I mentioned earlier, science was boring to me as a child. With prayer that I would learn and find it interesting as a homeschool mom, science has proved a tantalizing journey of discoveries. Hopefully, my children never think it's boring and are always poised to discover something new in the world around them.

CHAPTER 3

Selecting Curriculum

Joseph and Joshua homeschooling by "playing" games

Once you've determined a child's needs for the school year on paper, select curricula to meet those goals. When possible, ask several successful moms whose homeschool lifestyle you would like to emulate. Through the years, I have found some of my greatest ideas in networking with other like-minded moms.

This chapter includes the offerings of my experience with my children. Glean what you can from it. Certainly, curriculum should fit a mother as well as her student. For example, you may thoroughly embrace the teacher-intense style of Shurley Grammar. Perhaps your oldest is in mid-elementary. You have no high schoolers demanding your attention. But if your oldest two children are in high school, your daily schedule requires a great deal of you in numerous directions. Or if your oldest is a third grader, and you have four preschoolers, rigorous involvement on your part may demand more organization. Abeka grammar workbooks along with IEW writing might meet your needs better, as the workbooks enable independent work on some school mornings. With four children within five years of one another, this approach worked best for our home. Celebrate what works for your family. Remember, there isn't just one way to do many of these things.

One of the perks of homeschooling involves customizing each child's schooling to her gifts and limitations. Evaluate each of your children as described in chapter 1. Some are just interested in checking a box to meet a requirement. Each family will have to determine its goals. A mother with a special-needs child might focus more on skill building than on pursuing advanced reading. Or imagine a family who farms. The physical requirements of their lifestyle dictate that they plan their schooling around their manual work. A student headed for higher education in fine arts might take practical chemistry instead of advanced chemistry. Consider all the particulars in your home. In years past, I had the concerns of miscarriages, hospice for a nearby family member, and more than one family member struggling with cancer. Be pragmatic.

Begin by laying out the four core subjects. Establish what type of curriculum you and your student will use to best succeed for each. Although it may seem odd that I would mention "you and your student," the success of a school year often hinges on the way the mom and the student embrace their books. For example, if you love a discussion format for literature, you might devour Omnibus, which is a literature-, history-, and theology-based high-school program. Another option would have a student reading independently, answering questions, and taking tests. Some might want to do just the minimum in literature, while others might work to cover as much literature as possible.

Give thought to each subject separately. Start with the core subjects of math, science, English, and history. I like to start with math, as it can be somewhat tricky. My ideas are not exclusive to what might be available. The curriculum choices listed are all ones I would enthusiastically recommend. My desire is to be positive in the recommendations. Glean what might be helpful.

Math Curriculum Choices

Abeka—This math is my favorite choice for kindergarten through prealgebra. Once you add math word problems and manipulatives, work sheets, flash cards, and games, you have a strong math foundation for any student. This plan worked well for all my students.

Chalkdust—One of my children needed to see all the problems worked out the long way to be clear how to repeat the process, so this math curriculum helped as we approached prealgebra. When you watch the video with the math instructor, you might find yourself as distracted as I was during the demonstrations. He had the longest green chalkboard. If your student is self-propelled, she can work through this alone. If she needs accountability, you might sit nearby, stop the video, and work out the problem before the teacher completes it on the board. Overall, it is easy to follow.

Singapore—If your student notices how big textbooks or math books are at the beginning of the year, this might be just the fix. Many classically educated families who enjoy Sonlight materials embrace this math program. One of its best features is that the math is broken into separate booklets. Imagine completing a chapter or section and knowing that you've just finished a whole book. As you set it aside to move on to a new book, you feel a strong sense of accomplishment. Completing the bite-size portions of this material offers additional enthusiasm to many students. The material is thorough and prepares students for success.

Bob Jones University Press—Elementary workbooks are color-ful and exciting. Traditionally, these books present math a year be-hind the Abeka books. So you might want to work one level ahead if you plan to be in prealgebra by seventh grade. This company compiles high-school math to offer lots of extra practice.

Math-U-See—Use this program alongside Abeka or Bob Jones University Press, and you have a winner for any student who is a visual learner. The manipulatives with this program in the elementary years are just fantastic. I am not familiar with the high-school years, so you will have to explore those for yourself. One of my children would do the age-appropriate math each year from kindergarten through sixth grade in the first two months of school. Then she would switch to Abeka and complete every other problem until we reached about fifty pages into the book. Moving at this speed allowed us to catch up quickly with those who had just been doing Abeka from the beginning of the school year.

Free websites are everywhere. My current favorites include the following two sites.

Khan Math Academy—Everything on Khan Academy (https://www.khanacademy.org/) is just awesome. Some of my smartest homeschool mom friends love this site. A mom who is a retired navy fighter pilot is using Khan as her primary math teaching tool for her two children. Another mom moved to a new city in August as the school year was starting. After the move, the family did not have a permanent residence for about nine months. So, she kept her sixth grader working on Khan Academy through all the subjects listed for sixth and seventh grade. He transitioned easily to the new schooling situation.

Homeschoolmath.net—Look to this site as a resource for word problems, assessment, and work sheets. Certainly, there are many others like this one. Look around for one that suits you.

How to choose

Some things that should govern your choice include the following:

- Is the curriculum largely mastery based or spiraling? Is it spiraling with a short spiral like Saxon? A short spiral means that, in each lesson, most of the exercises are review problems. Often, a new concept is practiced only minimally within the day's lesson. Examples include Saxon, Abeka, and Horizons. Mastery-based programs usually are laid out in chapters that concentrate on a few topics, and then students do review problems separately. Examples are Singapore Math, Math Mammoth, Math-U-See, and Right Start Math.

- What is the cost? Check the websites. Sometimes you can buy materials used.

- Is it colorful or black and white? Some children like their material in full color; to others, lots of color is distracting. Similarly, lots of images might distract some children, while some children enjoy them.

- How teacher intensive is it? Does it require much teacher preparation? In many programs, part of the instruction is included in the teacher guide and part in the student textbook, so you have to go through both. Some programs employ videos for you to watch first.

- Is the curriculum scripted? Some parents like it that way; some absolutely do not, because they like teaching freely.

- Is the curriculum religious or secular? When it comes to math, this is usually not of major importance, because even if the publisher is religiously oriented, its math curriculum may not show it to any great degree since the math itself does not change based on how you believe.

Although I personally loved math as a student, I have only so many hours in my day. Once my students complete Algebra I, they join a math tutor in a small class or huddle. This group meets twice a week and tackles new concepts. Time does not allow me to teach, grade, and rework math for five and now four children. Each child learns math differently. One needs to see math, so Abeka and Math-U-See combined each year works best for her. Another grasps math quickly, making writing out the entire problem nearly impossible. Supplement your math learning with flash cards, bingo games, songs, online learning, and word-problem resources. The additional resources add variety and create a fun learning environment.

English

English—or language, as it is sometimes called—contains numerous components or areas of needed mastery. First, a younger student learns phonics to begin the mastery of the English language. This spurs reading. Read great books to your students, starting in preschool and continuing all through their development. Words and stories must delight, inspire, and motivate, so a younger student needs phonics and reading.

As a child develops, grammar, spelling, vocabulary, and literature comprise English. Use one source that combines all these areas, or be eclectic and put your favorites together. Also, some students need a combination of resources to best meet their learning style and needs. Some of my favorite resources for English development are given in the following section.

General English Curriculum

Five in a Row—This curriculum is literature based. Math, geography, relationships, art, and other areas are evaluated as the student reads a well-selected children's book once a day for five days.

Abeka Language—A choice that serves as a strong resource from kindergarten through eighth grade. This curriculum is a staple at my house for all these levels. The workbooks are colorful. They encourage mastery and provide all the practice needed to learn the new material. The great advantage of being a homeschool mom is that you have the prerogative to work through all the practice that you need or eliminate the extra work once your student indicates mastery. Time to move forward. Skip to the new material instead of drudging through something you already know well. As a note, we use Abeka language books for grammar and IEW for writing. So, we skip over any writing assignments in our language books. This skill is practiced elsewhere.

Sing, Spell, and Write—This excellent learning-to-read program combines song with spelling and sound rules. This is a mother-intensive program that I used for all but my youngest child. In early years, we completed this early in the morning along with Bible, language, math, and music practice. This approach will not be familiar to traditionally educated adults, but it is easily absorbed with just a little bit of preparatory study. Once you assimilate this approach, you will be delighted at the new things you will learn. As mentioned in other places in this book, homeschooling your children gives you the great benefit of reeducating yourself, which is a very exciting prospect.

Hooked on Phonics—This is the best source for a challenged child. The process is lengthy but thorough. It offers remedial work for children or adults. Although it was originally developed for adults learning to read for the first time, it works for any age. For most students, the repetition in this course might not be necessary. But it is worth looking at as a successful option.

On a personal note, I know two children who struggle with learning in a traditional setting who used this program successfully. One is a child with Asperger's who now reads well. My oldest also unintentionally used this program when I was teaching him to read. When he was in junior high, we discovered that he struggled with dysgraphia. (Dysgraphia is the inability to write coherently. Frequently, this problem is coupled with attention difficulties.) In the professional assessment that followed, the psychologist questioned how he had learned to read. She stated that he should not have been able to read. This astounding fact proved to me that even though he should not be able to read by professional-educator standards, he surpassed even normal standards of reading ability. In third and fourth grades, he read through our *World Book Encyclopedias*. This was unbelievable. His retention proved stunning. Over the years, he read books and articles voraciously. His first attempt at the ACT resulted in a score of 33. Although I don't attribute his success solely to this reading program, I would mention that it took me three hours each morning for a year and a half to complete this program with him. Patience and perseverance brought us success.

Get Ready for the Code and Explore the Code—Here are easy lessons to supplement your grammar in a solid curriculum. If your child is feeling sluggish or running ahead or you need to work with another student, pull out these books. Kids love them. You know they are educational. They support phonics and spelling. What's not to love?

Handwriting

As an aside to thinking about English studies in general, all students should be encouraged to include handwriting as a part of their daily routine. Taking just twenty minutes a day to practice forming letters and to refine their copy-work skills will assuredly add significant polish to anyone. My favorite picks for handwriting are Handwriting without Tears, Italic with Getty/Dubay, and Reason for Handwriting.

English Curriculum and Resource Suggestions Sorted by Grades

Preschool—Grade 2

Bob Books—Instant confidence boost for early readers. Each book homes in on one vowel sound at a time.

Spell to Read and Write

Reader and read alouds from Sonlight and Veritas Press lists

Abeka language workbooks

Lots of audiobooks—My favorite sources are Lamplighter, Odyssey, and books on audio from the Sunlight and Veritas Press reading lists. I love Audible for myself and for the children. Audiobooks are a dream for students who are eager to learn but struggle with reading.

Grades 3–6

Abeka language workbooks

Institute for Excellence in Literature (IEW)—Writing program for grades 3 through 12. My own children used IEW writing from grades 3 through 8. This encourages writing one to two paragraphs weekly while creating clever sentences. Patterns of using a thesaurus, a dictionary, and word lists become the normal writing habits of these budding students. They don't know anything different. Since I have taught this writing program for ten years, I have seen incredible progress in students who were eager to write as well as in those who were reluctant writers. Nothing beats this approach to creating excellence in writing.

Easy Grammar—Teaches grammar in increments. Use as a remedial source for students or as a review in grades 6 and 7.

Explore the Code—Use to complement primary source. These books are easy to work alone. Perfect for car school or while the parent is needed intensely with another child.

Shurley Grammar—Excellent grammar curriculum. Teacher intensive. Use with several grades at one time. Rote memory work is very important to future success. Although this program is outstanding in grammar, its writing program is not my favorite. Great success is achieved when combining this grammar with the IEW writing program.

Wordly Wise—Delightful vocabulary resource. Use for spelling too.

Reading lists from Sonlight and Veritas Press

Grades 7–12

Abeka—Grammar. This is my personal favorite workbook for these ages. We do them in grades 7, 8, and 10. My kids are usually at a level of mastery with these three completed.

Abeka—Vocabulary and spelling

Etymology such as *English Words from Latin and Greek Elements* by Donald M. Ayers. (This might be best consumed over two years. We aim for mastery, so it takes a little longer than most programs.)

1000 Words You Must Know—Flash cards with this program speed learning.

Institute for Excellence in Writing (IEW)—Writing program for grades 3 through 12

Omnibus I, II, III, IV, V, VI—Covers ancient history through current world history. Counts for Ancient History, World History I, World History II, and American History on transcripts. Combines literature, history, and theology for integrated learning.

Abeka—All literature textbooks

Bob Jones University Press—All literature

Sonlight—Recommendations

Poetry Collections

Remember, English as a subject is composed of grammar, writing, reading, spelling, vocabulary, and literature. Each of these subjects must be sorted into the school year. Generally, all these subjects are done weekly in elementary years. Once the student reaches junior high and high school, grammar and literature can be done intensively and alternately. Literature should be consistent or alternated with writing and composition. Some homeschoolers combine reading aloud in family time and appropriate-level reading assignments for time reading to them.

Literature

While literature falls under the category of English, it warrants individual planning. This topic offers delightful possibilities. Literature ranges from classics to short stories to poetry to philosophers to theologians and a range of other options. Literature is what we read when we finish our grammar. Grammar is harder and really more of a rote exercise, while literature encourages time together on the couch, an audiobook in the car, or a quiet corner at the end the school day. As you might sense, I leave reading assignments for the afternoon or car time. A good read allows for musing.

Much of the best literature should be read aloud together. Perhaps you sense my love of words. It's true. I am drawn to books and words. They seem to me a warm and intimate conversation with someone from another time or someone I might never meet.

When I write, I imagine that you and I have drawn up close beside each other with a cup of coffee or tea so that we might share our thoughts.

Science

Science offers many nontraditional learning options. One of my favorite is notebooking. Our family loves journals. Science notes can be kept in a notebook designated for learning a particular subject. For example, suppose your children are going to study birds for two months. Select a journal of appropriate size. Create a cover. Begin taking notes on what you learn from books and observation. Some students enjoy sketching or using items they cut out or print. Learn from online sources. Discover pages or photos to include in this study. Truly, this is an intensive approach. Remember that the traditional approach to science encourages a student to learn and repeat snippets of numerous subjects each year. An intensive look at birds, for example, gives the student a much deeper understanding of this subject. Usually, combining the reading and hands-on exploration creates interest and fun in many subjects.

Since I am homeschooling with a mind to continue homeschooling year after year, completing science with intensive study on one subject at a time means that I will complete all generally studied areas in most science textbooks and more. The key to success here includes vision and planning. As I mentioned earlier, some families take a year-by-year approach. If you envision long-term commitment, lay out a plan for the elementary years and the seventh- through twelfth-grade years. If you evaluate the subjects you want to master, you can set aside the big-picture goal and dive in deep on a single subject.

Since science was never interesting to me as a young person, I feel strangely excited when studying it with my own children. After a few years as a homeschool mom, it dawned on me that my newfound enthusiasm about science was because the textbook approach to this subject was excessively boring. Interactive science along with colorful resources is action packed. Did I mention that I am a field-trip enthusiast? Science provides a plethora of field-trip ideas. Spring and fall are my favorite times to capitalize on science-type field trips. Our area offers a botanical garden, a phenomenal zoo, a nature center, farms, numerous developed parks, and a hummingbird festival, along with a world of other opportunities. The world is waiting to be discovered. Literally start with your neighborhood.

Landry Labs offer two- to three-day intensives that encourage students to delve into lab work related to one category of science. For example, a lab intensive on biology would include dissections of various sorts, the study of cells with a microscope, and other related hands-on experiences. For students who completed work only or book work and labs at home, this intensive enhances the material. Whether selected as a review at the end of the studied material or prior to beginning the class, these labs deepen comprehension. If Landry Labs don't come to your area, recruit one of your favorite science teachers to present the science labs you need. Some of our best learning experiences are ones that we dreamed until they materialized.

Science Curriculum Suggestions

Apologia—Throughout all grades, these science resources are my favorite selection. Science resources from the other organizations in this list complement them.

Answers in Genesis (AIG)

Usborne

Dorling Kindersley (DK)

Bob Jones University Press—Texts

Potter School and Apologia—Online classes

Two- to three-day intensives to complement book study

History

This subject evaluation is the hardest to write because I *love* history and overdo on this subject consistently. Then again, can you overlearn history? When does a student or mom feel as though she is an expert on any section of history? The more I learn, the more I feel I don't know. The further I dig, the further I am inclined to dig. My curiosity never ends. Part of the excitement lies in reading biographies and true stories from history. Historical fiction places me back in history by recreating the culture and life of a time past.

The resources for history are vast. In most subjects, I can narrow my favorites. But the list for history is longer. Veritas Press and Sonlight catalogs undoubtedly rise to the top when I'm making my reading selections each year. Veritas Press created the Omnibus series for seventh through twelfth grades. My own children will likely complete four to five of these books during their seventh- through twelfth-grade years. These books are best taught in a Socratic circle. During many of the last ten years, I have taught or facilitated this class on Fridays. Students meet for hours as we discuss the books we read and the ideas they invoke. Complemented by essays, the Omnibus books are just the best for combining history, literature, and reading.

My oldest child took honors in college. Within the first month of his freshman year, he told me that honors seemed like our Omnibus class—only our Omnibus studies took him deeper into the material. During that semester, they read authors we had covered in Omnibus. Due to time constraints, there was not time to read about the background, author, cultural assessment, character development, and Biblical analysis for each book covered. All the other honors students he knew were not only unfamiliar with the books assigned but also found the authors unfamiliar from their previous educational experience.

Currently, I am teaching Omnibus on Fridays in my home with a huddle that includes my children and some of my favorite teens. One fabulous feature of this approach is that it embraces the learning of moms and dads with their upper-level students. Classes include a range of ages discussing and learning together.

To complement what we read in history at all levels, we incorporate the *Mystery of History* books. The best part of these books is that they are so conversational and appealing to the listener. Linda Hobar delights us all by personally reading the books on her audio resources. At intervals, we read the sections out loud. My children read the books to themselves. Also, we listen to the audiobooks. Road trips are always better with purposeful audio. Decide how your family can read and reread these books.

Whether you jump into homeschooling at the beginning of your students' education or somewhere in the middle, establish a big-picture plan. If schooled from kindergarten through twelfth grade, your student ideally will finish an intensive journey from creation through modern-day history four times before she graduates from high school. This requires a plan. Let's look at the idea of history from kindergarten through twelfth grade. Determine whether your family will cycle through history every three years or every four years. Many of my favorite resources sort history in one of these two ways. A simple approach might be to select one type of history curriculum and follow it exclusively.

Our family learns a section of history together each year. For example, this year we are covering the period from the 1800s through the modern day. My four students at home will use a variety of resources to track together on this plan. My older students have circled through history three times so far. My girls are covering history and literature together in the Omnibus VI book this school year. Our schedule for Omnibus is established by late May. My girls choose books from the first-semester reading list to read in the summer.

As we approach each history time, I look into my current selection of historical fiction. These books are selections from Veritas Press, Sonlight, and used books collected in my twenty years of mothering. The younger students, who are in sixth and seventh grades this year, will follow many books with the older high-school students. In addition, we will review Usborne resources, the Kingfisher history book, Veritas time-line cards, the time line on our wall, and other related time-line resources. Each student completes a book every one to two weeks.

Historical fiction is an unknown treasure. If your background is like mine, history might have seemed dull even to the best of students. As an A and B student, I found history monotonous. Historical fiction establishes the frame and culture of history, along with an individual story, to capture the attention of the reader. Once the reader bonds with the characters, he wants to understand the clothes they wear, a normal day in their lives, the people they interact with, the social norms of the day, and a myriad of other fascinating details. Like watching a great movie, historical fiction draws you deep into the understanding of the character's experience. In doing so, it allows the reader to absorb history, culture, and sometimes the moral strength of the character.

As a homeschool mom, I was determined to create appeal for every subject, never revealing my boredom or disdain. I approached each new learning goal with enthusiasm. In looking at history, I found historical fiction to be magnetic. Most of our read alouds have been historical fiction. Imagine reading historical fiction from the first century and then contemplating the lives of the people in your Bible. In my experience, scripture and history become three-dimensional through the window of historical awareness. Eager listeners during our family reading time often beg for one more chapter. Gotta love that.

History Curriculum Suggestions

Veritas Press—Books for all grades

Mystery of History—Books and audiobooks. This group of four volumes with short stories can be read out loud or alone. Complementary resources for geography as well as hands-on activities enhance overall learning. Do as an individual, family, or small group.

Sonlight—Books sorted by grades and reading levels into readers and read alouds

Lamplighter—Books and audiobooks

Tapestry of Grace—Best done in a two- to four-family huddle

Usborne—Books

Other Subjects

Geography

Undoubtedly, geography is one of my favorite subjects. For those who believe that context expands learning and comprehension, this subject is key to fully grasping current news, history, and literature. For those who love the Bible, the perspective of geography and history creates an almost three-dimensional effect on the true stories we read in the beloved Scriptures.

Geography Curriculum Suggestions

Geo Matters—This resource offers delightful materials to study geography. Geography resources abound. Because geography is considered such a minor subject for most students, geography curriculum is usually geared toward a semester study. Over the years, my children have completed several geography programs. We love geography. Using resource books, map apps, and drawing resources, my own children have developed a strong mastery of most geography. Reviewing geography curriculum proved more time consuming than I expected. Some resources focused on physical geography, such as the countries, cities, and physical features. Others focused on the culture and people of each continent. Consider using several sources to gain mastery. A few of my favorites are listed as follows.

180 Days Around the World

Geo Matters Resources

Bob Jones University Press—Geography resources

Abeka—Geography

Classical Conversations—Geography is interspersed throughout.

Over the years, my children have studied geography intensely. They have memorized hundreds of places and passed testing. This year, we are embarking on a delightful adventure in the subject. For about three years, I have been trying to make up my mind about how to create a comprehensive three-inch geography notebook for each of my children. My intention was to gather all that they have learned so far, review, and push it even further. After great deliberation, our notebook is under construction. For those of you who like to keep life simple, skip the next section. For those of you interested in my project, keep reading.

Comprehensive Geography Notebook

Our intensive geography notebooks will begin with a personally decorated cover. I recommend the Avery notebooks that have a cover allowing an insert. These notebooks have proved sturdy in the past. Their front covers can be folded back behind while you're working with them open. These notebooks will include a big-picture look at the entire globe, including physical geography such as water currents, air currents, topography, and weather patterns. The first tab will be for general information. Each of the next seven tabs will identify a continent and its nearby land masses. We will begin our journey through each continent with a delightful set of questions from 180 Days Around the World. Each student will insert previously studied geography, such as maps they have drawn and colored.

As mentioned before, my intention is to review what we know at the beginning of each continent study. We know most of the countries and their capital cities as well as land and water features, including rivers, lakes, peninsulas, and such. Most mountains, canyons, and trails are familiar. In our study, we also want to know about the people of these lands. What do they eat? What do they wear? Where do they live? What is a typical day like? What religions dominate? What has God done in these places in centuries past? Who are the missionaries past and present in these places? What is God doing there now? How can we pray for this land? What history has occurred in these places? What famous people lived on this continent? How has history lived in this land? Our family plans to carve out two hours a week to work on this study. I imagine it will take a school year, a summer, and maybe an extra semester.

Languages

Suggestions abound concerning language. My children work through Greek and Latin roots in their elementary years. In eighth and ninth grades, they meet with a top-notch Latin tutor who moves intensely through Latin. The intention is comprehension of Latin roots, conjugations, and translations and the general recognition of Latin influence on all languages.

My favorite curriculum for integrated Latin and Greek roots is an etymology course appropriate for high school by Donald Ayers, *English Words from Latin and Greek Elements*. For high-school credit, my students complete two years of Latin and two years of Spanish. My intention is to place them in a Spanish-speaking environment that forces them to be fluent in conversational Spanish. What is the point of taking Spanish or French or German or any language if we cannot read and speak it? If language is approached as all other subjects are, students learn the grammar of the language followed by implementation of its use. Some parents are also eager for their students to learn Arabic or Chinese. Each family will need to sort out their goals.

Logic

Many programs promise results in logic, but my personal journey is full of examples of what not to do in this subject. Along the way, I have found fabulous books that are entirely fun and practical for both moms and students.

Logic Curriculum Suggestions

Fallacy Detective

Thinking Toolbox

The Amazing Dr. Ransom's Bestiary of Adorable Fallacies by Douglas Wilson and N. D. Wilson. I highly recommend the flash cards.

CHAPTER 4

Preparing for Preschoolers

Silly Joseph - Love that face.

Make Preschool Years Count

Prepping for preschool is vitally important regardless of your school selection. Don't waste the preschool years by limiting your young one to entertainment. Maximize the season of learning that the younger years bring. While preparing intentionally for your preschooler seems like an option for the summer or school year, it should rank high in priority. Why? Because if the little ones don't have a plan to keep them busy, they will keep you from accomplishing your goals with the older children. Select purposeful activities and entertainment for the young ones to help them develop properly. Don't allow these formative years to slip away without making them count.

Think of the excessive television and other entertainment options that occupy the days of many young ones because moms neglect to select make better choices or because they are tired. Perhaps other children are demanding their mom's time. Young children, preschoolers in this instance, are in the prime of their memorizing stage. This is the time to train them to memorize, introduce them to a multitude of words through reading, create a love for books, play quality music (loudly and frequently), engage them in tactical skills, and just guide them to delight in the world around them. Let's explore ideas to nurture and optimize some of your little person's best years.

Memorization

Gather quality materials for them to memorize. We start early with Scripture in our home. Search for sources that include a picture with the memory work. The Scripture memory book we used in preschool years with all five of our children shows the verse on the left and the art piece on the right. Memorize Scripture by listening to songs. Volumes 1 and 2 of Steve Green's "Hide Them in Your Heart" continue to be among our favorites. Karen Henley's "My First Hymnal" CD and book also shine with excellence. I love all her resources. Write verses, frame them, and hang them on your walls. Place them strategically in the bathroom. Verses in these locations are always memorized quickly!

Bible Memory Goals

AWANA is hands down the best Bible memory program for children from third through sixth grades. Search for a healthy program in which children finish their books every year, and leaders are eager to help. Attend regularly. Work with your child to help him memorize at least two sections weekly. Study in the car. Study before bed. Study daily. Prioritize memory work. You will never regret this commitment. The young years fly by. Scripture is easily tucked into the memory early. Early memory is more permanent too.

Think of this: Would you rather have your children watch some meaningless movie or show over and over because you need an activity to occupy them? Or would you rather select music and quality memory work for them that enriches them at the point of intake as well as in the future?

Sparks AWANA group with Joshua to my left.

Quality Literature

High-caliber literature often comes in audio versions. Listen to an audiobook while driving, cleaning, or playing. Many libraries offer books on audio. Selecting books from a suggested book list promises more listening satisfaction than does random selection.

Poetry enriches a mom's life as well as the lives of her children. Currently, we are reading through an American poetry collection. Delightful! Kids thrive when their senses soar with purposeful literature. On a side note, some of our favorite children's books have been used for forensic speeches. Believe it or not, these speeches have made it to nationals more than once.

Since the older children were memorizing in eight academic subjects for school while the preschoolers were around, the younger ones absorbed all that memory work too. Committing poetry and selections from classical literature to memory never fails to enrich.

My preschoolers could also rattle off preposition lists, Latin verbs, multiplication, science, and Bible passages. While they were too young to understand it all, they were storing it for later, when knowing the grammar of a subject would accelerate their propensity for the subject. Just hearing quality literature read will increase their vocabulary.

Daily Boxes

Whether your preschooler is the oldest child in your family or one of the younger ones, having a plan always makes for a more successful day. One of my favorite ideas included dividing favorite toys into five separate boxes. Each box was then labeled for a day of the week. Monday's box might have included Duplos, a playful patterns game, several stuffed animals, crayons, two coloring books, and other favorite playthings. At the end of Monday's school time or playtime, the box for Monday would be put away.

The next day, the Tuesday box would produce new fun. So Monday's toys and activities could be played with only on Monday. They would not be seen again until the following Monday, making them more enticing. If all these playthings were available every day, they would lose their magic. The boxes housing these playthings were large and stacked in a corner of the room. Mark the boxes with the days of the week for additional excitement and extra exposure to learning them.

Educational Activities

A wide range of educational activities exists for the preschool age. A trip to your local school store will offer even more than your imagination can. Some of my favorite preschool tactical activities include stringing beads, board puzzles, metric patterns forming shapes, colorful frogs used for counting, and coloring books. Companies that offer high-quality items include Discovery Toys, Playmobil, and Usborne. Products from any one of these companies will likely be very difficult for you to part with when you have no preschoolers in your home. (Save them for your babysitting box or your grandmother box.)

Tactical Activities

Common items also work well for tactical activities. A shallow pail or cookie sheet filled with sand makes a great base for practicing letters and numbers. Sifting through beans or rice invites young ones to practice drawing shapes and letters.

Play-Doh is a classic form of entertainment. Just the smell of Play-Doh makes me happy. Give your child a sturdy plastic plate. Invite him or her to select a Play-Doh color. Give her a rolling pin and a few cookie cutters. Instruct your child to sit at the table and keep all Play-Doh on the plate instead of the floor. Even children as young as eighteen months can follow this directive. My experience is that parents and teachers often avoid this delightful activity because it is very messy. Confining the activity to a plastic plate or tray works beautifully. Any escaping Play-Doh risks the loss of creative privilege. This works with young preschool children. I can offer assurance of this because I have taught a class of twenty three-year-olds who kept their Play-Doh on their own plates.

Field Trips

In closing this section on purposeful preschool play, use your imagination in guiding your little ones to delight in the world around them. This begins when you delight in the world around you. I love field trips. Some of my favorite destinations include the zoo, the botanical gardens, parks, farms, and our own backyard. If you decide to do field trips with friends, take a vote on where the others would like to go. Plan purposeful fun.

Visiting Philadelphia with Josh & Joseph

Magnifying Glasses

We own a small collection of magnifying glasses in a variety of sizes. One of my favorite memories involves giving our preschoolers their favorite magnifying glasses and asking them to look at the ground around them. I set the timer for about ten minutes. No talking was allowed. Then we all gathered on a picnic blanket with snacks to discuss the interesting things we had seen with our magnifying glasses. Delightful and insightful! This activity is perfect for numerous locations and should be repeated over and over so that the children as well as the adults involved appreciate the minute wonders of the world God created for us to enjoy.

Preschoolers are naturally curious. They love to play. Almost any activity will seem like fun if an adult is interested in playing too. So don't neglect purposeful activities for your preschoolers. As you are restocking your van, spring cleaning your main living area, or selecting school items for your older children, think intentionally about your preschooler. Whether you are a young mom, a new mom, or a grandmother, think of ways to stimulate cognitive growth in your little person. Whether you are planning the summer or activities for the school year, search for books, DVDs, hands-on activities, workbooks, and effective activities for your sweet preschooler. Always remember to prepare purposefully for preschool. All ages benefit from reading or listening and absorbing words. Most children should read or be read to as frequently as possible. When my children were preschool age, we read to them for about an hour a day. They also listened to audiobooks. The artwork in a well-illustrated book tickles the imagination. Locate quality books easily by finding a preselected reading list from a reliable source. As mentioned before, my favorite sources include Sonlight, Veritas Press, and Lamplighter. Once you locate a favorite book, search for other books by the same author.

One of my favorite children's series is a set of books about border collies. The initial book, which is my favorite, was *Floss* by Kim Lewis. They include breathtaking watercolor sketches of border collies, which the author owned and loved. The delight of reading these books was split between the enjoyment of the art and the charm of the story. You could write an entire book detailing the charm of such children's literature. *Honey for the Child's Heart* is actually such a book. If you are approaching summer or the school year, consider purchasing this book or dusting off your bookshelf to search for new adventures for your young ones.

Another idea for prepping for preschool is to expose your child to music from numerous sources and genres. "Music is the voice of the soul" is a quotation written on the wall above our piano. Granted, we are a musical family. But all children benefit from music instruction and the exposure to music. The debate about whether musical ability is inborn or learned remains unsolved. Playing music in the background while a child is working or going to sleep undoubtedly increases his intelligence, creativity, and appreciation of the arts. So intentional exposure to music is a plus for all preschoolers. Music aids memorization. Music calms. Music charms.

My Katie and I have been teaching three-year-olds on Sunday mornings for two years. One of the little girls who has been coming to our class is most definitely on the autism spectrum. Early in the fall, she seemed oblivious to the other children and resistant to interacting with the adults. She wandered in her own world, interacting with various toys. She could not do any of the crafts. She could not color or use a glue stick. She failed to even stay seated during story time.

This semester we added more music and the guitar. Wow! On hearing the music, she suddenly connected with us. At first her words were unintelligible and her singing more like a monotone. Within a month, though, she was singing the words and staying just a beat behind us with the music. Many of our songs are straight scripture verses. Her mother spoke to us recently and asked whether we had taught her "Jesus Loves Me." She mentioned how her daughter sings with clear words many of the songs she is learning on Sunday morning. My point here is that you should be intentional when using your child's time during preschool. Teach scripture. Play music. Combine both. What a delight to know that music has reached the soul of this child and allowed us to bury scripture in her heart!

Select a variety of music. Take children to live concerts. Many concerts are available at your local gardens and arts museums. Play music for your child as she goes to sleep. When my children were young, I hunted lullabies. My favorite lullaby CD is *Sleep Sound in Jesus* by Michael Card. Mozart and Bach are available in numerous formats. *The Mozart Effect*, a CD set, is perfect for lulling babies to sleep or as background music for students.

CHAPTER 5

Whole Child

Selfie with Katie

Beyond Requirements—Developing the Whole Child

D o you dream about how to develop your child's gifts?

Do you desire that your child reach his or her potential?

Do you search for skill training for your child's current skills and potential skills?

Do you purposefully plan for the growth of all areas of your child?

Do you plan for the academic, spiritual, physical and social maturity of your child?

Do you often wish you could guide your child to success in all areas of life?

Does your child need to develop socially by thoughtfully selecting new friends?

Does your child require attention for an academic problem?

Do your child's skills invite ongoing opportunities to improve? If so, look for people with master skills who he can shadow. Search for classes and camps that will grow him.

Do you need to schedule a doctor's appointment to chase down a mysterious worry?

Most importantly, do you need to cancel parts of your schedule to allow more time for reading and maturing your child spiritually? See the recent article on "Spiritual Blooms" on my blog at www. nurturingmynest.com.

Like all parents, homeschool parents approach the time of year when students take standardized tests, the ACT and SAT, and final exams with some trepidation. While we are attempting to successfully complete the spring semester, the final decisions about the summer and fall semesters beg completion. Yet decisions for your child are not limited to academic ones. If you are like me, planning can be overwhelming. As a mom and homeschooler for more than twenty years, I have developed a system that really works for us. If you need a new strategy for evaluating and decision-making, see if this idea works for you.

Assessing Your Child's Strengths and Weaknesses

Effective planning involves assessment that comes from watching your child's behavior and accessing written testing. As a parent, you likely observe your child's strengths and weaknesses in academics and in other areas such as church and social opportunities. Knowing your child's strengths will provide insight to his weaknesses. Yearly testing with standardized tests updates you on your student's place among his peers and on the appropriate expectation of his maturity with subject material. All of this may be altered if the child has a learning difficulty or if another extenuating event occurs.

For example, say your student scores poorly in homophones. That sounds silly, but it happened to me. I noticed that the test included eight questions. My child missed six. That might indicate that we need to work through some of these words, or it might mean that she does not know those six words. It might also mean that she was hungry and it was almost time for lunch. My point is that these tests are helpful, but do not worry too much. Grab the information that is helpful. Work on your child's weak areas, but use your mother's intuition if you feel that one of the test numbers is not correct.

Noticing that the student missed only seven of the twenty questions may clarify this part of the test. Perhaps a yearly or biannual extensive evaluation best benefits both student and parent. End-of-the-year evaluations in each subject are usually more useful in highlighting mastery and deficiencies. Academic plans often dominate a homeschool mother's thoughts during the spring season, but pause for a moment to think about all the parts of your child. Evaluate your *whole* child.

Twice-a-Year Evaluations

Taking a meaningful look at your child's progress in all areas of growth twice a year will keep you on an intentional evaluation.

When changes are necessary, plot out a route for change. Often these times of reflection cause me to remember something that I meant to do but simply forgot. This habit is not difficult to cultivate. Here are five easy ideas to fully grow your child.

Five Ideas for Developing the Whole Child

1. **_Locate a place for intentional planning._** This brainstorming stays behind a tab in my day planner. Other ideas include a file on your computer or in your desk area at home. Return two to three times each year to look over your child's progress and preplan for the upcoming season. The year seems to be broken into three parts for us—fall, summer, and spring. Each of these requires a transition in the schedule, so rethinking these areas is part of the process.

2. **_Select a page in your planner that identifies the academics, spiritual, physical, and social areas of each of your children._** In order to flesh out this idea, I created pages for two children in the example that follows. Personalize each child's needs.

Child 1—Age Eleven, Entering Sixth Grade

Academics

Bible—Awana Bible-memory club

Music—Piano lessons

English—Language VI

Spelling VI

Writing—IEW

Literature (Sonlight)

Math

Math VI (Abeka)

Math games/speed drills

History

Mystery of History—Book I

Books from Veritas Press

Books from Sonlight

Science

Apologia Zoology IV

Apologia Anatomy

Usborne Science Encyclopedia

Spiritual

Writing Bible verses in personal Bible journal in the morning

Family Bible time

Awana

Apologetics cards for speech club

Serving in Sunday-school class for three-year-olds, car care for widows

Physical

Recreation with Dad

Sports teams—Soccer, basketball

Social

Learning to cook

Eating smart

Friend time

Child 2—Age Fourteen, Entering Ninth Grade

Academics

Bible—One chapter daily

Music—Piano lessons

Flute/piccolo

Voice ensemble

English—Language IX, 1100 Words

Writing speeches/literature

Math

Geometry

History—Omnibus World History Geography

Science—Apologia Biology

Spiritual

Personal devotions

Family time on prayer

Names of God

Apologetics

Serving

Sunday worship for kids

Mission trip?

Physical

Soccer

New pediatrician

Swimming (WSI)

Social

Driver's permit

New healthy friends. (Aim for two new friends.)

Contributions around the house

(For more, see the blog "Teaching Children Chores" from www.nurturingmynest.com.)

3. ***Review written tests***. Sometimes standardized tests reveal trouble spots. Anything that is deemed remedial can be done first thing in the morning. Sometimes a certain subject is just going to be challenging throughout a child's education while other times a subject can be brought up to grade level with concentrated effort.

4. ***Pray as you consider each area of development.*** Ask God for insight about the child in this time of growth. Seek solutions to areas of need. Search for your child's friends.

5. ***Celebrate progress.*** These times of reflection give confidence that aimlessness is not behind the next step. Purposeful thought and movement always produce the best result. Ask God to help you visualize the needs of your child in the next growth period.

Plan to take your child out for a special time including her favorite food, such as ice cream or sushi. With discretion, talk through all the progress that you recognize she has made this past year. Share your dreams and plans for the upcoming months. Remember, you have prayed for God's direction in your child's future.

Communicating how precious your child is to you and to God will motivate her as you inspire her to grow successfully as a *whole* child.

Now I'd like to address why developing a child spiritually is so important. A pressing question for any devout Christian parent might be how to impart a love for God in a unique, growing child. One might ask how a child will be prepared to participate in the church body as an adult. A child needs to prepare as he is growing from child to adult. Any parent who loves the Lord personally should consider how to communicate spiritually with his child. Many stories recall the failure of this transfer. Think of Samuel in the Old Testament and how he failed to reproduce children who loved God as he did. Think through the kings at the end of the Old Testament. Some of them chose to follow God. Others, like Josiah, honored God even though they had no guidance from the adults who came before them. Although a parent may pour into a child who rejects Christ, the responsibility of spiritual training rests on the parent in the home. Many leave the role of raising a child spiritually to her activities at church. My point is that each of us should intentionally teach our children to read the Scripture and pray daily. Teach them to sing the Scripture. Create a love for journaling their favorite verses. Teach them to sing spiritual songs, worship songs, songs of today, and hymns of yesterday.

Dream of the passions that you would like to instill in your children. Then be intentional in sparking those passions. My heart is strongly drawn toward children and missions. While my girls were in high school, we took two mission trips to India to lead children's conferences. The impact of planning and traveling and of the experience will likely live in their hearts forever.

India mission trip

Teaching at a women's conference in India

Imagine your child as an adult in the body of Christ years from now. What training or experience will your child need to participate successfully in her church? Consider your child's gifts. Provide opportunities to work with children, to lead music, to serve meals, to clean up rooms, to take out the trash, to set up for services, to learn puppets, to be a clown, to help with VBS, to organize recreational games, to serve at a reception, to learn a sound board, to take pictures, to make posters, to collect for someone who has lost his job, to mow a lawn for a widow, and to serve in other ways. Access training in teaching children, such as child-evangelism fellowship or storytelling. Be enthusiastic yourself about serving. If you have a heart of kindness toward others, your children will mimic your enthusiasm.

Sadly, many adults are nervous when asked to teach a Bible story to children or adults. What an advantage a child will have if given this experience as a young person! What joy he will experience at the delight of a child enjoying the story being told! How a teenager will rise with maturity when placed in leadership! Knowing young ones will keep an eye on your decisions and motivate wiser choices. Some personalities may not gravitate toward teaching children or leading music in any venue. But they may be wildly talented with a camera or behind the scenes. Pray for God to reveal your child's gifts. Develop these gifts in the body of Christ as well as at home.

Pursue opportunities for your child to serve. Serving at home, at church, in the community, and possibly on a mission trip will instill innumerable values in your child. Serving others encourages our mental activities to pursue the needs of others rather than our own needs. Serving regularly encourages creative thinking and problem solving. Some find it's easier to pursue mission trips rather than weekly serving opportunities. Both are beneficial. Serving in your own home to your own family builds a child in an even deeper way. I've heard it said that you are who you really are at home. Commonly, people struggle to get along with their family members but find it easier to serve others outside the walls of their home. Nurturing the family unit and culture is truly more important than serving outside the home if one has to choose. My home is certainly no perfect example of serving and selfless living, but it is our intention to instill those values in our children and have them lived out at home.

CHAPTER 6

Schedules

Discussing schedules could consume several books. So much has been written on how to organize a school schedule. If a mother takes her students to a traditional school setting and drops them off, she then has several hours to run errands, grocery shop, and clean house. At least time without the children is available to her to use at her discretion. Working mothers consume this time by going to their jobs. A homeschool mom's children are always with her. Her home is occupied more during each day than are the homes of many other families. All things considered, for a homeschool to work smoothly, the school schedule must be organized along with home maintenance.

Check out the following two resources for home organization.

Emilie Barnes's 15 Minutes a Day

www.flylady.net

Or Google "homeschool" and "organized." You will discover a plethora of ideas. Below are ideas that work at my house.

Organizing the Home

Domestic jobs such as laundry, ironing, cooking, cleaning, large cleaning jobs, home maintenance, care of a baby, and a myriad of other tasks can be completed efficiently by a team helper. This necessitates Mom patiently spending time on the front end instructing how to complete a job. Just this week, my oldest daughter was attempting to teach her eleven- and twelve-year-old brothers how to iron a dress shirt. Both these young men take joy in dressing up. Since they are eager for their clothes to be ironed, I thought it was time for them to learn how to iron their own dress shirts.

Once my daughter began to teach them the process of ironing a shirt, they were stunned at how long it took. She was equally surprised that the teaching process was lengthy. Lesson one completed. A four-by-six-inch card near the ironing board listed the order in which the parts of a dress shirt should be ironed. One lesson in ironing will not make a successful job. But if we work at this training a few more times, the boys will gain a new skill. This work will be transferred. Eventually, my boys may own the job of ironing their shirts instead of having them dry-cleaned or expecting their future wives to do the job for them. Few things are more attractive than a domestically efficient young man.

Many moms feel too tired to train their children to do these domestic jobs. Let me encourage you, though, that however tedious the training period for a domestic chore, a successful result will always be worth the time invested. Many resources suggest age-appropriate chores. Some suggestions follow.

But let me suggest that the term *contributions* replace the term *chores*. Semantics count. The word *chore* implies drudgery and duty. *Contribution* communicates teamwork. *Contribution* also implies the value of the contributor as a necessary player. Just try it. This might be part of the contract that you draw up as you begin each school year. Decide on what you expect and what you will contribute. Put this on paper. Meet with your student. Read and sign it together.

The following list by Sheila Seifert from Focus on the Family spurs you in the right direction.[6]

Age-Appropriate Chores

Do you know what chores your child can do? This question is somewhat answered by Sheila Seifart in a recent article published in Focus on the Family. What chores are important for your children to learn, and what are they capable of doing?

First, recognize the difference between a chore (an ongoing task that benefits the household) and a life skill (an activity that children should know how to do before living on their own, such as managing a checking account). The following list does not include life skills. It is a list of chores.

Second, remember that every child matures at a different pace. Adjust this chart to what you know about your children's skills and talents, and realize that no child should do all the chores listed below every day.

With those two qualifiers in mind, here are some general guidelines for personal and family chores. This list is only meant as a guide and reflects the types of chores that many children in these age ranges are capable of completing:

Ages 2 and 3

Personal chores

- Assist in making their beds

- Pick up playthings with your supervision

Family chores

- Take their dirty laundry to the laundry basket

- Fill a pet's water and food bowls (with supervision)

- Help a parent clean up spills and dirt

- Dust

Ages 4 and 5

Note: This age can be trained to use a family chore chart.

Personal chores

- Get dressed with minimal parental help

- Make their bed with minimal parental help

- Bring their things from the car to the house

Family chores

- Set the table with supervision

- Clear the table with supervision

- Help a parent prepare food

- Help a parent carry in the lighter groceries

- Match socks in the laundry

- Answer the phone with parental assistance

- Be responsible for a pet's food and water bowl

- Hang up towels in the bathroom

- Clean floors with a dry mop

Ages 6 and 7

Note: This age can be supervised to use a family chore chart.

Personal chores

- Make their bed every day

- Brush teeth

- Comb hair

- Choose the day's outfit and get dressed

- Write thank-you notes with supervision

Sadie & Katie

Family chores

- Be responsible for a pet's food, water, and exercise

- Vacuum individual rooms

- Wet mop individual rooms

- Fold laundry with supervision

- Put their laundry in their drawers and closets

- Put away dishes from the dishwasher

- Help prepare food with supervision

- Empty indoor trash cans

- Answer the phone with supervision

Ages 8 to 11

Note: This age benefits from using a family chore chart.

Personal chores

- Take care of personal hygiene

- Keep bedroom clean

- Be responsible for homework

- Be responsible for belongings

- Write thank-you notes for gifts

- Wake up using an alarm clock

Family chores

- Wash dishes

- Wash the family car with supervision

- Prepare a few easy meals on their own

- Clean the bathroom with supervision

- Rake leaves

- Learn to use the washer and dryer

- Put all laundry away with supervision

- Take the trash can to the curb for pickup

- Test smoke alarms once a month with supervision

Ages 12 and 13

Personal chores

- Take care of personal hygiene, belongings, and homework

- Write invitations and thank-you notes

- Set their alarm clock

- Maintain personal items, such as recharging batteries

- Change bed sheets

- Keep their rooms tidy and do a biannual deep cleaning

Family chores

- Change light bulbs

- Change the vacuum bag

- Dust, vacuum, clean bathrooms, and do dishes

- Clean mirrors

- Mow the lawn with supervision

- Babysit (in most states)

- Prepare an occasional family meal

Ages 14 and 15

Personal chores

- Responsible for all personal chores for ages 12 and 13

- Responsible for library card and books

Family chores

- Do assigned housework without prompting

- Do yard work as needed

- Babysit

- Prepare food—from making a grocery list and buying the items (with supervision) to serving a meal—occasionally

- Wash windows with supervision

Ages 16 to 18

Personal chores

- Responsible for all personal chores for ages 14 and 15

- Responsible to earn spending money

- Responsible for purchasing their own clothes

- Responsible for maintaining any car they drive (e.g., gas, oil changes, tire pressure, etc.)

Family chores

- Do housework as needed

- Do yard work as needed

- Prepare family meals—from grocery list to serving it—as needed

- Deep cleaning of household appliances, such as defrosting the freezer, as needed

Adulting

A few years ago, my sixteen-year-old daughter came to me with a list of domestic skills that she felt she needed to learn before she left home. She listed a few things that I thought she would feel efficient completing currently. We intend to complete the list ahead of time.

My mother taught me all domestic skills before my senior year in high school. The summer before my senior year, she asked me to be responsible for our home for a month. Although I knew how to do everything she was asking, I was very concerned about whether I could do it all at once. My responsibilities included laundry and ironing, planning the menus, shopping at the grocery store within our budget, organizing the meals, preparing the meals, cleaning the house weekly, monitoring daily straightening of the house, and keeping one vehicle clean.

Now this daughter is married, and I am confident that she is completely ready for the domestic challenges of her life ahead.

Initially, I struggled to organize these skills. Sometimes meals were late. Sometimes most of the meal was ready, but the food got cold while we waited for the rest to finish cooking. Laundry was easy. No trouble with it. I was taught to fold warm clothes coming out of the dryer before reloading both machines. Overall, I learned to think through the time and manage our home efficiently.

Katie's wedding day

Throughout college and even entering marriage, my confidence was high that I was prepared for the task ahead. If you gauge the activities that vie for your attention in your adult years, domestic activities grab quite a bit of that time. Why not be properly prepared for the tasks that will be expected of us?

Establish goals that will create an independent adult. Invest the time necessary to train your child to do all the domestic jobs he will need to complete as an adult. Teach the boys all the domestic jobs. Teach girls yard work and maintenance. If we serve one another at home, we will better serve others away from home.

Thanks, Mom, for training me and trusting me. What a gift!

What High Schoolers Can Contribute to a Homeschool Day

Select their course of study—especially electives.

Develop a lesson plan.

Plan and teach a unit study.

Present a lesson to a younger sibling.

Grade papers.

Read aloud.

Create a schedule with weekly, monthly, and yearly goals.

Give a dictation or spelling test.

Direct a hands-on math lesson.

Help occupy younger siblings during lessons.

Perform domestic jobs such as laundry, ironing, cooking, cleaning, large cleaning jobs, home maintenance, care of a baby, and a myriad of others.

Teaching Your Children to Organize Their Activities and Time

Part of parenting involves organizing teamwork. As your student develops into a teenager, involve her in understanding what is required to complete high school. When considering academic goals, show her the requirements as well as the elective options. Allow her to select electives, online skill-building courses, and intensives. Currently, my daughters are interested in learning more about photography and playing the guitar. As we approach the summer months, we intend to watch numerous online instructional videos on both these topics. As mentioned earlier, once we complete the requirements for high school, only six collective options remain. So, the extra classes and training that we pursue will be listed on our academic résumé. Mostly, we love to learn.

Develop a lesson plan with your teenager. Schedule a day out with your teenager that will allow you to work through a schedule for the academics and other activities for the fall or summer. Last year, I took my teenage girls out to a nearby Vera Bradley store to select their own day planners. Prior to our date, I printed the academics we would cover in the upcoming school year. The subjects were listed in order of importance, along with the number of hours needed weekly to complete the assignments.

Next, we talked through possible outside activities they might add to our schedule. We added music lessons. Mutually, they decided to be active in our speech and debate club and a Christmas play at church. As we considered our serving options, the girls opted to play music at a cancer-treatment center and teach a Sunday-school class for three-year-olds. In the fall, we sell products at several venues. We selected these venues that day. Once we had a clear picture of our choices, the girls began to sort these activities onto their weekly calendars.

Think of the benefits of a child growing up and having the opportunity to organize her responsibilities and activities. Without this experience while growing up, they will be forced to learn many of these skills quickly in adulthood. Some adults opt to skip the learning of basic skills altogether. They either pay others to do them or just leave them undone. Once my daughters completed the job to the best of their abilities, we noticed a few areas in which they might need to adjust the time expectations. Overall, I was very pleased. Sometimes I have to make changes in my initial plan for a schedule, so it was a natural expectation that they would need to make adjustments as well.

Planning Three Parts of the Year

Consider that there are three sections to any year—two semesters and summer. Most people enter these sections of the year haphazardly. Set aside some planning time at the beginning of each of these transitions. Consider the work and play you wish to accomplish. Coming into the summer, determine your daily, weekly, and monthly goals.

Our summers are intentionally relaxing and home focused. We want to be in the pool, eat at home, enjoy the activities around town, read a load of books, catch up with friends, and perhaps squeeze in a unit study. As the kids age into teens, they sleep in later in the summer if they do not work an early shift at their jobs. Since my husband and I wake up early regardless of the season, we enjoy quiet reading and visiting time while drinking our favorite freshly ground coffee.

Prior to cleaning out the schoolroom, I sit with my day planner detailing each child and his or her needs. Read chapter 13 for details on this planning. Most of the elementary subjects are taught here at home, with the exception of a writing class, which I teach them and others elsewhere. In high school, my children go to math and Latin tutors. All other subjects are taught here. This necessitates intense planning on my part. My tendency is to select the hardest subject to plan first. Once all subjects and curricula are selected, I search for used resources. By the end of May, whatever I cannot find a used copy of, I purchase new.

Some families seem to struggle with the cost of books, whether these are textbooks or reading books. Consider this: Public-school attendees still incur costs for a variety of items. Participants in band or sports must purchase uniforms and other items. Private-school students' costs go beyond tuition, uniforms, and fees. As I plan for my school year, I am overwhelmed with choices. Once I have made my selections and shopped for them, I don't stress about the cost of the books. Any investment in books is an investment in the minds of my children.

As a side note, I encourage traditional-school parents to purchase books from many of the catalogs we enjoy as homeschool moms. I find it quite alarming that a large number of parents trust the public-library system to offer books of value for their children. Consider the worldviews of those selecting books for the library. Visit your local library. Peruse the shelves. This experience should convince you to purchase reading material intentionally for your children. If you feel financial strain when making book purchases, consider the value in the development of your children. Most people easily spend money on sports or a hobby, so book purchases should be even more deserving of financial allotment.

Schoolroom Reset

At the beginning of the summer, I sort through all items in the schoolroom. My goal is to touch every item to determine whether we can get rid of it or share it with a friend. One narrow bookcase in the schoolroom contains a cubby for each child. While I'm cleaning up in May, I fill each of these cubbies with academics for the next year: all-new textbooks, workbooks, learning CDs, extracurricular books, new notebooks with tabs, and learning tools. I select many items for resale. I sort work from the previous school year into notebooks. Each child has a three-inch notebook full of his or her elementary work. High-school accomplishments are stored in another three-inch notebook. Once the schoolroom is cleaned out and ready for the next year, I am ready for summer.

Summer Unit Studies

Teens are great at planning unit studies. Kids love working with students who are just a bit older. As you know, young kids think older kids are very cool. So, this plan is actually beneficial in both directions. The older student practices planning, teaching, and implementing, while the younger students enjoy being taught by a teen. During the planning process, aid your teen by supplying resources and ideas. If he is teachable, help him complete his planning by thinking through where problems might occur. Start with a brief unit study.

For example, decide to plan a family meal. Designate a leader, your teen, who will select a date, plan the meal, devise a table setting, and organize his team. If you are preparing a meal for my family, using any recipe requires math. I mean multiplication, as most recipes feed about four not-very-hungry people. Shopping for the meal while using your teen to prepare and implement it will prove to be an excellent learning experience.

If your teen is musical, she might want to organize new or prepared musical pieces into a presentation. Music interspersed with Scripture and some interpretive reading makes a delightful gift for an assisted-living home or a widow.

Teamwork

As your teen matures, she is capable of presenting a lesson to a younger sibling. When you have numerous children, the older ones often have a schedule that dominates. In our family, we find ourselves traveling frequently to tournaments in the spring. Although we progress rapidly on academics in the fall, the spring academics necessitate greater creativity and energy.

Our family finds it necessary to pair up the children on road trips to these tournaments. In my case, there are two older girls with two younger brothers still at home. Each sister is paired with a brother. Usually we begin the day with math. The lesson is explained, guided, and graded. The girls do their own work while helping their younger brothers succeed. This keeps everyone on track.

Joseph & Riley

The boys can even help their older sisters with school. One of my younger boys is excellent at giving spelling tests. One of our family goals is to work as a team. Don't you think that one reason God put us in a family is so we can learn teamwork? Most days, this goal presents an uphill battle. But cooperation is worth striving for.

Older children giving dictation or a spelling test to younger siblings help Mom's load. Reading out loud so that another can complete his oral work offers insight into spelling, grammar, and comprehension. This beneficial activity also gives practice in note taking for lecture settings. Spelling and vocabulary tests for each child each week can account for many hours, especially if you insist on grading each test promptly. Offer practice for teamwork by having your students assist one another with dictation and tests.

Grading

Grading is one of the ongoing responsibilities of a homeschool mom. As the years have gone by, I have shared this monumental task. Give careful thought to your grading needs. Consider those who are available to help. My children often tackle the same science and history. This makes it easy for them to exchange lessons and to grade the completed work between each other. Although I'm careful not to overload my teens with helping tasks, I find they are willing to help grade as long as we stay fairly current. We grade tests promptly, generally within two days of completion.

Reading Aloud

Reading aloud to younger ones is a joy. Since reading quietly and reading aloud are ongoing daily activities at our house, everyone pitches in to help. We have family reading time frequently. Reading aloud is not just for younger children. We consider it a delight to be read out loud to, no matter what age we are. Unashamedly, I admit that reading time is my favorite part of schooling my children at home. It certainly is one of my favorite activities to do as a family.

Have no illusion that everyone will sit quietly and cooperate with your goal of reading out loud as a family. Anyone who tells you that all her children sit quietly for reading time may need to offer a demonstration. Be assured all effort on your part to read together is worth it. Keep active children busy with Legos, knitting, crocheting, coloring, drawing, or ironing. Busy hands make attentive minds. Whether reading a Lamplighter book, a poetry collection, a volume of historical fiction, a music-history book, or a story from a recent blog, reading time rates as highly valuable.

CHAPTER 7

Extracurricular Activities

D on't overdo.

Homeschoolers these days are tempted to overdo all the wonderfully enticing extra opportunities. With outstanding field trips, exciting classes, sports, music, speech, debate, and more, a mom must be determined to stay on track with her goal of completing the core academics first. Travel opportunities for sports and other exciting groups tempt moms to choose the fun extra stuff instead of the grind of core academics.

The lifestyle of homeschooling offers the freedom to be productive without numerous interruptions. It also embraces the freedom to slow down and smell the roses. At our house, this might mean spending some more lazy time with our furry friends.

Most students find some subjects easy and others difficult. Some years, most of our outside activities have been eliminated due to the need for extra time in a problem area. One of the perks of homeschooling is that you can identify a deficiency in your knowledge or skill and work toward bringing it up to mainstream level.

Maximize Field Trips

Over the last few years, homeschoolers have gained an upward spin of respect in their communities. In our area, homeschoolers are truly catered to at museums, the zoo, and science locations. When we call to book a field trip, we mention that we educate at home. This usually opens additional classes for our students. They know we will come prepared by studying the material they send us. Sometimes they send a teacher study guide with pertinent information concerning the upcoming lab or field trip. If a teacher desires her class to gain the optimum learning experience, she teaches her students the suggested material in advance.

For example, let's say that your group is going to visit an art museum for a particular exhibit. To maximize student learning, you teach them about the artist's background, show his or her works, and discuss his or her art style. This orientation promises that the students will build on a foundation of material once they go on the field trip instead of going in cold without any information. Layering the learning promises greater retention.

Musical Opportunities

Most homeschoolers find a plethora of music opportunities. Private lessons, band, choral groups, theater, and contests offer more options than a student can realistically participate in. When sorting options, gratefully consider that you have a smorgasbord.

When selecting musical options, deliberate on long-term goals. Personally, I feel that piano is the basis of all music training. Once a student applies herself on the piano, she acquires strong sight-reading ability. Competency involves music theory and rhythm in addition to sight-reading.

At my house, we take piano through sixth grade. Then we may add an additional instrument. Those taking the Suzuki method may find that reading music later in elementary school leads you to be just as successful in music as a traditional approach. The result varies from teacher to teacher and student to student. Regardless of the path, competency is the goal.

It seems, from numerous sources and personal experience, that music builds skills in math, reading, and memory work. Ideally, a student continues to study music throughout his academic years. Some of mine added voice or an additional instrument. Perhaps the most problematic time to continue the discipline of music is in the junior-high years. Encourage ongoing music training. Musical skills usually do not develop much past the stopping point in high school unless a student continues training into college years. The skilled musician grows if she participates in music regularly as an adult. So work hard while the time to mature is available.

If my adult children actively participate in music in their local churches, nothing will please me more. Music ability complements children's programs as well as adult events. Leading worship music for any age group is a great joy. Many instruments complement that effort. Playing music lends itself to so many great opportunities. My daughters play the harp and flute in addition to the piano. We share our gifts by playing for a cancer center and other worthy causes. Patients coming to receive chemo and radiation are gifted with heavenly instrumental music in the waiting room. The girls have played for weddings, events, and dinners. The paid opportunities encourage them to keep up their repertoire and use their years of practice as an opportunity for income.

Sports

My family only participates in recreational sports. This may change, however, in the future, as both the younger boys are eager to play baseball more than just eight weeks in the spring. Many of our speech and debate friends are fully involved in traveling for sports as well. Homeschoolers usually can play any sports they desire. A few exceptions exist. Many scholarships for individual sports such as golf go unclaimed every year. One of my pediatricians shared that he only taught his four boys individual sports. He felt that although team sports were fun, individual sports could be played far into adult life. Many individual sports offer a ticket to college as well as a strong connection when doing business.

If your student is interested in a particular sport, start asking everyone whether there is a place for a homeschooler to be involved in the sport. Networking is likely the best way to gather information. Sports camps offer connections. And although sports have their place, remember that the most important thing is raising a child who pursues godliness and is kind to others. Don't neglect family time or spiritual development for a competitive sport.

Joseph # 53, playing for the Memphis Nighthawks

Josh playing football with the Nighthawks – Fall 2017

Sports should be primarily about learning to play on a team well, sportsmanship, and growing up to be a better man or woman. Being an encourager who is loyal to the team can be an invaluable lesson. Learning to lose gracefully is certainly just as important as learning to win with grace and humility.

Theater, Speech, and Debate

Theater opportunities abound. One of the advantages of being a home educator is that you have a more flexible schedule. The disadvantage in this situation might be that the flexibility of your schedule means that some people view the school part of your day as optional. Regular bedtime and a strict schedule ensure that the student can enjoy a positive theatrical experience while not getting too far behind in school.

Speech and debate competitions offer even greater value for strengths to take into adulthood. Skills required when competing improve a student for any occupation as an adult. Giving a successful speech flows from brainstorming, writing, editing, adding more quality words that best express the idea, timing, absorbing the evaluations of others, crafting a title and conclusion, considering your audience, and the unspeakable value of competing. The National Christian Forensics Communication Association (NCFCA) and Stoa offer national tournaments for homeschoolers. Your location determines which league offers communities and competition in your area. Each group brings unique areas of competition to the student. If your student competes with excellence, she will gather the best result from the invested time. This is true of any activity.

With Katie & Mikayla at a speech and debate tournament

Debate competition stimulates development of research skills, listening, value assessment, refutation, sportsmanship, cross-examination, and more. Some students are naturally drawn to debate, whereas others would be mortified to compete in something requiring an impromptu response. Such vast differences in response exist in my family. Some love impromptu speaking. Others don't. Some love interpretive speaking, while others prefer platforms. The skills acquired in the experience of debate competition, however, will greatly enhance future success. My intention is for all my children to compete in debate for at least one year. Others intend to debate throughout their entire high-school careers. Each area advances different skills.

Regardless of your students' natural skills or your comfort level, encourage them to be involved in speech and debate competitions. Words are inadequate to describe the personal development acquired in this exercise.

Travel Opportunities

Look for educational opportunities when traveling. If you can leave a day early to peruse a museum or festival, make it happen. Search for camps and experiences that enhance your child's learning opportunities. My kids have been to marine biology camp, debate camp, a STEM science competition, science fairs, art exhibits, aquariums, geological outings, national parks, zoos, art camps, sports training events, and a growing number of other adventures.

Bubble tea in Kona, Hawaii

CHAPTER 8

Networking

Everyone benefits from developing the skill of networking. If you are a homeschool mom or dad, networking remains one of the best ways to acquire information and contacts. How does this play out regarding the topics discussed in this book? Imagine you are just beginning to homeschool. You google the word *homeschool*, and in a second, 17,700,000 results pop up. Wow! Where do you start?

I suggest you look around and see whether you know anyone who is homeschooling. You might take the person out to lunch and ask her what she likes best about it. What does she wish she had known before she started to homeschool? What are the best things she's done while homeschooling? What programs or resources does she recommend? Ideally, there will be several homeschool moms you can take to lunch. Select moms whom you want to emulate. Not everyone is worth copying. Avoid needy mothers who are not initiating making their own choices but are just following those of others.

On a regular basis, I find myself searching for new information in order to homeschool better or organize my home more efficiently. Just this summer, I have been in hot pursuit of information about colleges, scholarships, and SAT testing. Since we visited colleges and asked questions, we have learned the questions we need to ask. Although my oldest is already in his junior year of college, successful with his 33 ACT score and full academic scholarship, my girls' needs and interests are different. So we are pursuing information and experiences. We pray for insight. We pray for direction. We pray for answers.

This networking exercise reminds me of replacing my carpet with wood flooring about two years ago. I had never had wood flooring in my home, but I had cleaned wood in other homes. So the beginning of this journey included asking those I knew with wood flooring what they liked and didn't like about the flooring in their homes. Next, I visited three showrooms and asked them to sell me on their wood flooring products. I asked why their product was better than that of their competitors. Continuing on my quest, I acquired three bids and spoke with potential installers. All this gave me a clearer vision of what to select for our home, what to expect in the installation, and how to care for our floors. I believe that asking what others liked and disliked about their wood flooring made our decision more thoughtful and wise. Our installer was awesome. I love our wood floors. Apply this idea of networking to the things you need to know about in educating and raising your children. It works!

Another subject consuming my recent inquiries is geography. As discussed elsewhere in this book, I am interested in creating in my children a love for all the people of the world. Information about current cultures seems easy to acquire online, but I am looking for more. Where do I find the mission heart operating on each of the continents in our world? Many church resources orient their mission-outreach groups to a foreign country. We already have access to the information from three of these ministries because I asked questions.

Whether you select private school, public school, or homeschooling for your children, build a list of intentional things you want to teach and do with your children before they are grown and gone. When you don't know about something, ask around. This is how you learn too.

Imagine that you have started a new job. You need to train in your new skill in order to be proficient and successful. If you are just beginning homeschooling, whether you have a four-year-old or a fifteen-year-old, you should inform yourself about home education. This involves networking by meeting other homeschool moms who are successful. Think of other things you have wanted to learn. Collect successful ideas from those who have implemented them. Avoid mistakes that others warn you against.

When you need to locate the correct material for classes, ask others. Are you searching for materials that can be used across several ages? Do you need material for a child who has a unique learning style? How does a recommended teacher operate in the classroom? Is she more traditional with the use of textbooks, tests, and quizzes? Does she promote more essay writing? Do previous students like her? Is she organized? Does she communicate well with the parents? How much do various classes cost? Are there any hidden fees? Look at stacking outside activities onto one or two days a week. Recommendations from other parents are really the best determiners of quality tutors to supplement your homeschooling.

Networking with other homeschool moms also provides encouragement and a realistic outlook on your efforts. If you remain isolated, your expectations might be discouraging. Realizing that others struggle in maintaining a schedule, motivating students to complete assignments, and selecting curriculum gives you a better sense of normalcy.

CHAPTER 9

Selecting Classes

U sing outside classes to supplement your efforts at home requires consideration of costs and benefits. Most outside elementary classes range from one to two hours weekly and cost between $250 and $400 per year in our area. High-school classes meet between one and three hours weekly and range from $400 to $600. Cost should not be the primary deciding factor when selecting a class. As we all know, some environments are more efficient for learning. Once again, references really count when selecting classes.

Outside classes are available from kindergarten through twelfth grade. On an elementary level, writing classes and science classes are popular. Many choose not to begin outside classes until high school. Numerous factors affect these decisions. If a student lives quite a distance from class, travel time may affect the decision to take the class or to access an online class. Today, classes for upper-level science and history usually follow a more college-bound approach. Students preparing for challenging academic colleges are best prepared with quality science labs along with other intense classes. Some moms teach the subjects they feel they can master or the subjects that don't require a master tutor at home. Some subjects are easily self-propelled.

If you want to supplement your student's education with outside tutoring, ask around for classes that meet your goals. Ask young students what classes they have taken. Did they like the course work? Did they like the teacher? What was the best part of that class? Granted, some children dislike all learning. But you will find helpful information when you ask students about their class experiences.

Ask moms about the communication from the teacher, about the grading system, and about how wisely the time in class was used. Once you identify quality tutors, stick with them. Sometimes I make my selection based on the relationship of my student with the tutor. For example, my daughters love their math tutor. Since the curriculum and material covered are high quality, the situation is a keeper for as many years as we need a math tutor. As I mentioned, I usually keep math at home until Algebra I. Then, because of the time constraints of teaching five children, they master math with an instructor.

Outside classes don't have to meet weekly. Some rigorous learning offers a one-time experience. One-day intensive or weeklong trainings offer the benefit of concentrated learning. Even a focus for the summer months offers immense benefit. Immersion in a subject has great advantages over brief periods of learning in numerous areas.

Art is this way for our family. Over the years, my children have attended arts camps and one-day and half-day art experiences as well as a weeklong camp at my house. My mother-in-law was a phenomenal artist in numerous mediums. She pursued this interest after her children were gone. Her art teacher, Norma Dennison, just happened to live an hour's drive from my house. Being the delightful woman that she is, she and I had engaged in conversation many times.

One day, I had the idea of inviting her to teach classes for five days during the summer. Norma and I decided she would stay at our home overnight and teach the younger children for two hours in the morning while instructing the older children for three hours each afternoon. I put the word out. Both classes quickly filled with eight students each. That week of art proved delightful in all ways.

Training for the ACT involves cooperative efforts too. Although we incorporated practice tests in our materials throughout the year, several like-minded parents joined me in creating a huddle of four to six students for intense study. We met weekly for six to eight weeks or for half or full days during the week prior to the ACT. Although training both consistently and intensively adds to the students' skill development, doing a combination of both is often best.

Music and sports benefit from outside classes as well. My boys recently engaged in intensive baseball instruction. Training focused on batting, teamwork, and specific positions. My player who is gifted in catching spent an additional ten hours improving his catching skills. The boys worked with college athletes and coaches during summer break to improve these skills.

My daughters work diligently on their music skills all year round. Last year, I spotted an opportunity for my young harpist to meet a veteran harpist from Israel. With a concert and demonstration, this day of intense training proved excellent. She heard tips on performing in public, ideas on being prepared to share your music whenever asked, how to share your instrument with children, and how to deal with stage fright. She also heard about the lifelong love of this artist's harp.

One of the most memorable stories this harpist told that Saturday involved her volunteer work at a children's hospital in Israel. Many harpists are hesitant to allow anyone to touch their harps. Being close to a real harp is magical for children as well as grown-ups. When visiting these sick children, this harpist regularly invites them to play a song with her. Remember learning a simple pattern of notes on the piano while sitting by a more accomplished pianist who filled in the tune with an impressive flurry of keys? Her experience with these ill children is much the same. She teaches them a few easy notes and then plays a beautiful myriad of other strings around them to create a very complicated tune. The children are delighted, charmed, and mesmerized. For a moment, they forget their illnesses. So while my daughter learned how to play the harp more proficiently, she also gained an idea of how to practically share her music with others. Invaluable!

The school year also offers opportunities for your student to learn from a master teacher. Because I assume responsibility for my students' education at home, I eagerly access the expertise of master teachers. Once again, my goal of being at home and not overloading our schedule with outside activities comes into play when deciding about these classes. Most years, our family is out only two days a week. Protect your schedule by being home to homeschool.

Sometimes we slip out late in the afternoon after schooling at home for our music instruction. This gives us three stay-at-home days for completing schoolwork, family reading time, lengthy music practice, home contributions (formerly known as chores), and a yummy dinner. These are the kinds of days when we start a large pot of soup before breakfast. Soup is ready for lunch with a crisp salad and for supper with fresh, homemade bread. Don't you love being home together?

CHAPTER 10

Huddles

Huddles are one of my favorite ideas that I like to share. Perhaps you have never heard of a huddle. Imagine a team in a huddle as the coach or team captain builds spirit and camaraderie. Some of my ideas seem best implemented with accountability. Long ago, the idea of not being able to accomplish an important goal without accountability frustrated me. Now I think it is a brilliant tool.

Creating a Club to Accomplish Academic Goals

Perhaps you have been using the idea of huddles without even knowing it. Early in my homeschooling, I discovered the Veritas time-line cards for Bible and history. These cards are brilliant. I wanted my children to know the Bible, history, and art with the correlating information on these cards. However, there are 160 history cards and 160 Bible cards. As I do when tackling any lengthy goal, I divided the cards among the weeks of school. At home with the cards in front of us, I found it easy to linger and chase rabbits when covering this information. Not that digging in deep and lingering is a bad idea, but I did want the children to gain all the information on the entire set of these cards.

My solution to picking up the speed was to invite one of my favorite friends, Jennifer Higgins, and her two children to join us in a history club. Somehow, calling an academic activity a club appeals to children. Granted, we also always worked on crafts and ate really yummy food. Not surprisingly, our children remember the food the most.

Prepare Presentations

Initially, Jennifer and I met for an extended lunch and mapped out the school year. Our plans involved completing eighty cards in the fall semester and eighty cards in the spring. By meeting once a month, our club convened three times a semester. Club meetings included reviewing the cards selected for that month along with a craft or activity appropriate to the history covered in the time prior to club. All club meetings also involved a snack, of course.

Our students ranged from kindergarten through fifth grade. We met on a Friday afternoon once a month. Each of the five participating students brought his or her presentation on four-by-six-inch cards. These speeches included visual aids and posters to explain the topic further. Jennifer and I intended to read a large number of history books listed in the Veritas catalog. This time offered the children an opportunity to complete their reading and prepare a book report. The students read three books a month to themselves. Our families read one or two books out loud during family reading time each month.

Fun, Food, and Friendship

Today, the two oldest boys are in college. My two youngest boys, who were babies that slept during history club, are now in high school. Students from both families agree that this is one of the best memories of our homeschooling experience. Although club time was full of fun, food, and friendship as we met at my house, Jennifer and I were also delighted to meet our goal of reading through all those time-line cards in the two years we met for club.

Huddles seem to work best with two to four families who make up groups of three to eight children. They accomplish great learning together. Programs that complement this type of experience might be Tapestry of Grace, *Mystery of History*, a Veritas Press history and Bible time-line-card club, a science club, an art class, a chess club, a Lego club, a sewing class, or an ACT prep class. Imagination is the limit.

Share the Work

Let me give you another idea for a huddle in reference to science. Say you want to study botany for one year with your elementary-age students. Perhaps you select the botany textbook by Apologia and gather other books on botany. Find a friend or two or three with children of similar ages. Map out how you want to cover botany over the semester or school year. Meet every other week to discuss the designated chapters and do experiments together. Team mothers could divide up the weeks so that the families rotate bringing and demonstrating the science experiments pertinent to the chapters read.

Meeting on an afternoon late in the week ensures that core schoolwork is not interrupted by club time. Perhaps the mother or mothers who are not doing the science experiment can bring the craft or snacks for that club time. Most certainly, your students will work hard to be ready for club time. They will read their botany book. A club mother can do the science experiments or have the students take turns demonstrating them. The kids will have playtime with friends. You will meet your goals. Doing a huddle is brilliant in all respects.

Choose Like-Minded Moms

In proposing this idea, I must caution you to select a mother or mothers who are reliable and like-minded in preparation. If you like to prepare things with great detail, choose mothers who have the same style of schooling. If you desire a more relaxed approach, don't ask a type-A mom to be your partner; select a mother whose pattern of learning matches yours. Avoid choosing someone unreliable. Nothing is more frustrating than working with someone who is sloppy or who cancels on you at the last minute. You will be unhappy. It could even cost your friendship. All things considered, like-minded fellow huddle members will have a happier experience overall.

Huddle in the Summer

Huddles are excellent for accomplishing summer goals. One of my consistent goals during the summer is to read out loud to my kids and to have them read to themselves. Enthusiastic readers are usually motivated to read heavily in the summer because of the relaxed schedule and abundance of unstructured time. Sometimes a reading contest can motivate those who are reluctant readers. If you want to add to the motivation to read, consider a book club for your students with a few of their friends. Establish reading goals. Determine rewards. Plan play days or club time as rewards for those who meet these goals. Think of the perks this activity offers. A book club can be fun during the school year or during the summer break.

Friday Huddles

My Friday huddle allows for a three-hour discussion class as we review the assigned reading material for history and literature in our Omnibus class. Our morning begins with exercises in etymology followed by an overview of the week's reading, student essays, and lively discussion. Students love sharing what they have learned and reading their essays. Accountability pushes us to accomplish great amounts of material. The day is full of interaction, thought-provoking ideas and opinions, snacks, and friendship. So, we accomplish our goals together, on time, and with excellence. Gotta love it!

Accountability

So, in closing, if you find yourself struggling to accomplish a goal, consider a huddle. Or if working with accountability sounds like a great way to secure success, think huddle. Pray for the right group to huddle with as you work hard to learn.

Plan ahead. Share the work. Celebrate learning with friends.

CHAPTER 11

Car School

One of the easiest and most productive habits a mom can cultivate for noticeable success is implementing car school. Whether you homeschool or choose to do school in a traditional way, you likely realize how difficult it is for your child to sit still to memorize, read, or listen. Some children are naturally bent toward these behaviors, but many are not. Because I have succeeded wildly with this idea over my twenty-plus years of parenting, I vouch for it enthusiastically!

Car school may be a novel idea to some. Early in my parenting, we started memorizing Scripture verses in the car. It seemed easy enough to work on these while we were driving. We moved to listening to audiobooks, Odyssey stories by Focus on the Family, Scripture songs by Steve Green, geography songs, and math songs. Time spent in the car meant purposeful accomplishments. As the children developed academically, we matured into memorizing all sorts of academic lists, which established our knowledge of the grammar of a myriad of disciplines.

Five of the Best Things about Car School

1. Memory work is accomplished easily because the children are strapped in seat belts and want to hurry and listen to the audiobook.

2. Children listen eagerly (and quietly) to audiobooks. (Gotta *love* the quiet!)

3. Happy kids make for a happy mom.

4. Kids are distracted by purposeful activity, so they are not pestering one another or whining.

5. Learning done in the car does not have to be accomplished at another time outside the car.

Learning Activities to Do while in the Car

1. <u>Bible memory work.</u> Use AWANA for kids ages two through twelve. Join an Awana club, and watch your child easily memorize God's Word. Use Bible memory cards, and work together as a family. Make your own cards. Memorize a passage of Scripture together. Memorize Scripture that helps with character that you want to improve in your home or your life.

2. <u>Scripture.</u> Many offerings of the complete Bible on audio are available. Listen to this in the car together. We use these on road trips or early mornings.

3. <u>Audiobooks.</u> We love Lamplighter books, anything Odyssey from Focus on the Family, Narnia, and Jonathan Parks adventures.

4. <u>Math.</u> Problems can be done orally with flash cards, wrap-ups, or songs.

5. <u>History.</u> This is one of my favorites. Currently, we love *Mystery of History* and Henty books. The possibilities are endless in this category. Audiobooks can be expensive, but consuming this knowledge with speed and ease is worth the cost.

6. <u>Literature.</u> Look for a reading list that you love. We love the Veritas Press and Sonlight lists. If your child attends a traditional school, there might be a suggested reading list. Locate the audiobooks for these recommended books at your local library, on Audible.com, or through another online site. Just a tip: when we find an author we like, we start hunting other books to read by that writer.

7. <u>Grammar.</u> —While it sounds boring, many resources offer grammar basics set to music. Nothing makes this subject easier to learn.

In order to be successful with this plan, you will have to resist the temptation to turn on your favorite music. But investing this time in your kids will prove worthwhile. While this last idea is not exactly school, it can be done when in the car. Planning or having family meetings in the car proves very effective. Your audience is forced to be still and attentive. Much is accomplished. Consider car school as a new option for car time with your kiddos.

CHAPTER 12

High School and College

Simpsons 2014

When discussing high school and college, I still feel like something of a novice. My oldest son schooled at home for twelve years. After he secured a full-tuition scholarship, he joined the honor society and maintained his 3.6 GPA. He entered his third year of college as a senior and has just moved into his first apartment. Whew! I can't believe that information belongs to a child of mine. Somehow, my own high school and college years don't seem that far in the past. Perhaps you shake your head and feel the same.

During my years of homeschooling, I have watched with sadness as many fellow moms approach high school and college with little planning. Sometimes this means their students do not go to college at all. Other times they want to attend college, but they approach this time unprepared, without an ACT or any plans to pursue their dreams. Opportunities are lost. While I am certainly not an expert on high school or college, I will share a few thoughts that experience and networking have taught me.

Beginning at the end of elementary school, give serious thought to high school goals. Consider math. Determine whether your student is college bound or headed for skills training at a trade school. Experts encourage you not to make decisions in high school that would keep your student from having the opportunity to attend college. One possible track for math would be intense review of basic skills, preparing to complete prealgebra in seventh and eighth grades. A college-bound student might best benefit from taking Algebra I in eighth grade. This has the benefit of allowing the student to repeat Algebra I in ninth grade if necessary. Another thought is to review with prealgebra in seventh grade for the first semester and then begin Algebra I in the spring of seventh grade. This allows students to take three semesters to complete Algebra I. This extra time allows the students more time to solidify the concepts that make up the foundations of algebra.

Planning Junior High and High School at the End of Elementary

What I am suggesting is mapping out junior high and high school at the end of elementary school. Determining what your student intends to accomplish in high school as she is entering junior high will allow time for proper decisions. In our state, eighth graders are allowed to take two classes that will count on their high school transcripts. A thoughtful and purposeful jump at this opportunity in eighth grade will allow your student to finish his requirements for high school early enough to take AP classes, dual credit, and CLEP testing. The perks of planning ahead include more time to prepare for college, the opportunity to take classes in the student's interest areas, and a greater likelihood of securing his best scores on the ACT and SAT. Students participating in extracurricular activities that they love find more free time when proper planning is in place.

Leah & Mikayla

Securing a Strong GPA

As students begin to march through their high school years, a grasp of how their GPAs will affect their future choices encourages them to do their very best. A quick assessment allows both the parents and the students to look at their decisions about potential activities with a big-picture perspective.

Securing a Job? Volunteer Work?

Joshua with Levi & Tahoe

Will your student have a job to return to when school allows at Christmas and summer breaks? Is your student well rounded, as evidenced by a variety of experiences? Does she volunteer? Does she show responsibility and leadership in organizations?

Purposeful use of free time will develop your student spiritually, in skills, in personal relationships, in working situations, and in leadership opportunities. Spending time with family members as a group and individually is so important in these fast, fleeting years. In my home, we work hard to build memories and spend time together, as we know the day is coming when our children will be adults.

Shadowing

Students considering their college majors might benefit by taking a few days to shadow one or two individuals who are currently working in their field of interest. This experience lends itself to conversation about the day-to-day experiences in this career. A student might discover that the career path he is interested in is very different from what he imagined. He might discover a more efficient way to prepare for this career. He also might discover that this career path is not for him. What a gift to avoid wasting time and money preparing for a job that the student would not enjoy! Encourage your student to speak with people in his field of interest and ask what they like best and least about their jobs.

An academic résumé that accompanies the student's transcript offers your student the chance to place some of her achievements in front of college admissions personnel to determine peer scholarship opportunities. Your student's academic résumé will reflect her academic accomplishments, awards, volunteer work, athletic achievements, and work experience. Build a résumé that reflects your child's accomplishments. Although this information could be determined by looking at the transcript or perhaps in the college application or interview, this format quickly brings the information to the attention of the recipient. Such a résumé can be used to secure scholarships, acceptance at a university, or even a job. Those looking through applications view so many that your student needs to use something to stand out from the rest.

Selecting Colleges to Visit

As I mentioned before, I feel that I am still a rookie when sorting out colleges, intended majors and minors, and scholarships. Factors to consider include proximity of college to home, cost, field of study, student life, career development, and more. When selecting a potential college, the student's field of interest must be one of the guiding features. Find out which colleges stand out in that field.

Currently, my high school girls and I are visiting college campuses. In the last six months, we have visited seven schools. Some campuses were selected based on proximity to our home. Usually, in-state schools offer more scholarships. Others were in the vicinity of our travels. Still other colleges seem to offer training specific to my girls' interests. At this point, the decision seems to have circular motion. Some are noticeably awesome in one area and lacking in another.

It has been some time since I was a college student, and many changes have occurred in all aspects of college life. Most noticeably, the cost of college has increased 300 to 400 percent in the last twenty-five years. Fields of study seem to be broader. Specified tracks or minors listed underneath each major are called concentrations. Some universities are outstanding in offering direction for students looking for jobs after graduation. My alma mater certainly promoted its students to eager employers.

How Long Should a College Visit Last?

From our experiences this year, we have determined that a proper visit takes us a whole day. Allow three hours for the college visit. This usually includes a tour of the facilities, dormitories, and classrooms. Sometimes visitors are shown a film. Most visits end in a conference with some admissions officer who can answer financial questions. On most of our visits, we have also requested to visit with a significant member of the school that we are interested in. On our last college visit, we were privileged to meet with three deans. The dean of each department is usually aware of specific requirements for incoming students and potential scholarship money. Most admissions personnel we have met have only general information about acquiring scholarships. So, if my girls want to apply for scholarships related to their skills, such as music scholarships, they would need to be in contact with the dean of the music department in order to find out whether funds are available for scholarships and how they are doled out.

Some questions to consider when selecting a college follow. The order of the importance of these questions is yet to be determined in my mind.

1. <u>How close is this college to our home?</u> My second child is very interested in being able to drive home for the weekend when her studies allow. Secretly, this mommy heart would love that. But we must make a decision that is right for her for all good reasons.

2. <u>What majors or areas of study are available at this university?</u> This brings up the comparison of larger universities to smaller ones. We are still determining the pros and cons of small colleges versus large universities. Recently when we visited a large university, we were delighted to discover that they are strict on capping the number of students in a classroom, since a low student-to-teacher ratio is an advantage of smaller learning institutions. This added a point on the pro side for this sizable university. My second child has interests that are quite narrow. She might be better trained in the skills that interest her in an internship or online studies; it's hard to know at this point.

3. <u>How much will it cost to attend this university or college?</u> It's hard to know whether this question should be at the top or the bottom of the list. Since being debt-free is one of our family goals, we are not interested in incurring debt in order for one of our children to earn a degree. Looking for a university or college early allows us to explore what the university wants from us in order

to grant us scholarship money. My oldest is currently in college with a full-tuition scholarship. The girls are in high school, so plans are developing as we work to put ourselves in the best position for scholarship funding. This is another area in which networking is key to a favorable outcome. I have taken several moms to lunch or coffee to ask their advice. A university usually offers scholarships for specific academic programs or for artistic or athletic talents. As you investigate these routes for assistance, you need to know how to apply and qualify for these awards. Each scholarship committee looks for different things. Determine how you need to weigh in to secure the best award for your student. Planning ahead and networking could decide your student's future.

4. <u>How do we best prepare for success in the college years?</u> Obviously, that little number attached to ACT and SAT testing matters greatly. While I am opposed to teaching to the test, it is imperative that our students do their best on these tests. In addition to doing our regular schoolwork, we take practice tests and work with a tutor in the areas in which we need to increase our scores.

As a general rule, a student with strong reading and math skills will score high on the ACT and SAT. Target weak areas. To make sure your students are prepared with their best ACT scores for college, start Algebra I in eighth grade. This paces students to have completed math by eleventh grade, which puts them in a great place for success on these tests. Unfortunately, the success of securing scholarships and opportunities for college is greatly tied to the ACT score. A high score often leads to success when applying for college admission and funding.

5. <u>How is this college or university unique?</u> Ask students as well as admission directors this question. A current student or graduate has no financial motivation to give you the right answer. An admissions director has the job of selling you on his campus and might be inclined to give you only positive answers.

6. <u>How many students transfer to another school after the first year?</u> If the transfer rate is high, inquire as to the possible causes. Is the enrollment up or down? Be informed about the statistics of the school. You just might learn something interesting.

7. <u>What are the dorms like inside?</u> Ask to see all styles and configurations of dorms. Usually prices vary based on the size of the room, the number of roommates, and the location of the housing. Incoming students will probably place this question near the top of their concerns.

8. <u>What is the spiritual atmosphere within the student body?</u> Ask admissions personnel and faculty, along with current and past students. Will you select a Christian college or university or a secular institution? Choosing a Christian environment does not ensure a healthy

spiritual atmosphere. Have no illusion that a Christian selection will necessarily include a student body pursuing Christ with honoring behavior. When determining whether to send your student to a secular environment, ask what Bible studies are well received in the community and what churches students attend.

As my oldest was going to college, a wise man said, "A student will pick people of like-mindedness. If he is looking for quality friends, he will find them in any environment. If he is looking for friends to grow beside spiritually, he will find them. If he is looking for trouble, he will find it. If he is looking for the wrong friends, he will find them." Truth!

9. <u>What is the average GPA and ACP of accepted incoming freshmen?</u> This is an indicator of the academic standard of the institution you're investigating. If your student is academically challenged, select an environment with less rigorous demands. My goal as a parent is to find places where my child can be successful. Don't we all want this?

10. <u>Are freshman classes taught by professors or graduate assistants?</u> The quality of a class taught by a professor versus that of one taught by a graduate student is obvious. Considering the cost of college, select a higher-quality educator.

11. <u>What are the student demographics like?</u> Are there more boys or girls? Typically, colleges have a greater female

population. Are the students from public or private schools? Are the students from one area of the country? Other countries? Number of students transferring from community colleges? Students living on campus? Off campus? Gather any information available.

12. <u>What kind of job-placement programs are available for graduating students?</u>

13. <u>Have tuition and room and board gone up significantly in cost since last year?</u> If so, why? What do students think about the food? What food is available late at night on campus?

14. <u>How long have the deans and teachers held their positions?</u> This is a question that fascinates me personally. The ensuing conversation usually indicates enthusiasm and contentment with his or her position. On one occasion, it was clear there was some conflict in the academic environment. This question proves insightful and worth asking.

If change in the department is imminent, you need to know. We visited a college this year only to discover that the most appealing program at that school would be closing in the upcoming year due to cuts in funding. Knowing this steered us away from this choice. Determine how faculty is selected and tenured. Loving your faculty in college makes a world of difference in determining the benefit of your education.

Visits to potential universities have revealed more than we could have imagined. Strangely, our initial questions led to more questions. But even visiting a college that we eventually determine is not the right fit has filled us with a clearer understanding of what we are looking for in a higher-education institution.

Recently, we celebrated the graduation of our first child from college!

T.J. college graduation from Union University – One of our proudest days

One outstanding resource full of practical ideas is Ann D. Howell's *The Future Belongs to Students in High Gear: A Guide to Students and Aspiring Game Changers in Transition from College to Career.*

CHAPTER 13

Organizing Your Homeschool Space

What would you change about your schooling space?

What do you need to create more productivity daily?

What would increase your efficiency?

When your space is organized, your determined routine flows smoothly. Since homeschooling is hard every day, why not make it easier by improving function for you and your kids? Devise spaces that generate better results with cheery colors, fun storage, and clearly placed school items. Perhaps some of these ideas will help turn your school days into more pleasant, streamlined hours.

Determine Your Work Areas

As you consider your home and the ages of your children, determine where school might best work in your home. If your children are young, the school space might need to be situated near the kitchen and laundry room. Thinking through how your mornings function offers wise ideas on the placement of your school space. Most days, school is done in our schoolroom or in the living room. Our family gravitates toward the outdoor patio when the weather is gorgeous in fall and spring. Younger children might enjoy school in the early part of the day at a designated table, while later they might pile up on the couches for reading.

Sort Everything into Piles or Boxes First

Once the curriculum and resources are gathered, decide how best to organize each student's materials. For some time, we have used fold-up tables so we can change up the arrangement. Each student benefits from gathering her supplies. This may include items such as sharpened pencils, markers, colored pencils, scissors, math tools, and a variety of table and Post-it products. Needs vary based on age and courses pursued. For many years, necessary items were stored in plastic boxes with the color selected by the child and marked with the student's name. Each compiled a pencil bag for travel with his backpack. Taking time to prepare and keep needed resources at hand supports a smooth day focused on learning, not on searching for the right item.

Once all books and resources are sorted out for each student, choose a storage box or basket to keep things handy and organized. Some enjoy bright rooms with colorful storage, whereas others prefer neutral tones with black and brown. Whatever you select, just having a plan creates a sense of direction and order.

A tip for large families involves selecting a color that belongs specifically to each child. This eliminates stretching the mother's memory when identifying a myriad of items. For example, Child 1's pencil box, storage box, and notebooks would all be yellow. Child 2's items might be blue. Child 3 might be given green. This system often extends itself to the cups in the kitchen and other areas. Some view this as a way to simplify, while others might be overwhelmed. As with all ideas, settle on ones that make things easier and just pass by those that complicate.

Find Bookshelves, Baskets, or Storage Containers

One year for my birthday, I asked for eight bookshelves. My husband found this curious. However, bookshelves were just the solution to promote order among my school supplies and always-growing personal collection. Many companies offer bookshelves, but my favorite hands down are those from IKEA. In addition to being sturdy and versatile, they are priced surprisingly lower than many inferior choices. My husband drove me to the nearest IKEA and bought eight bookshelves. One of my clever boys put them together. The schoolroom was rearranged and resorted. Happy mom!

If you are schooling from your kitchen table, locate storage baskets or bins that meet your needs. Every day when you finish with school, take a few minutes to put everything back in its place. Some use a cabinet with closed doors. Others place matching baskets back onto a nearby shelf. Whatever works for you and your space, do it. Granted, sometimes it takes several adjustments to figure out what really works. Just keep tweaking your situation until it flows.

Group by Ages, Chronological History, Subjects, Core, or Supplementary Materials

When contemplating your school needs, you may want to keep just this year's items out. Some like to box up and store away anything that might not apply to this year. During the school year, I often think of something that I need from my stash. It's great to be able to access it quickly. Just today, I thought of all my books on Pearl Harbor. Because of an upcoming situation, I wanted them to read through these. They were handy, thanks to the IKEA bookshelves.

As schooling requires a multitude of items, the organization of the books and resources continues to change. Over the years, we have tried many ideas here, but we settled on the organization that follows.

History—chronologically from Creation, ancient, Greece, Rome, medieval, Renaissance, American, world

Science—encyclopedias, singular-subject books, kits

Literature—classic, must-reads, series of classics, poetry, Shakespeare, books for young children—for our pleasure, for speeches we write, for young visitors, and for babysitting opportunities

Art—history, how-to books, various media, various collections from famous artists

Missionary—favorite biographies

Biographies—These are mixed into other categories.

Resource books—dictionaries, thesauruses, encyclopedias

Audiobooks—a sizable collection for a struggling reader and for the enjoyment of us all

Other areas include those in the following list.

Extra paper

Writing tools, pencils, Expo markers, rulers, crayons, colored pencils, erasers

Calculators

2 x 3 cards, 3 x 5 cards, 4 x 6 cards

Puzzles

Games

Memory cards from previously retained material

All schoolrooms need a copier and an electric pencil sharpener. This is truth!

Sell, Give Away, or Donate Extras

Once a year, I go through all items in our school space. As my youngest is now doing all high-school material, so many levels have been completed. Cleaning out is very emotional, but it must be done. This year, eight boxes left this space for a used-book sale, to be shared with friends, or to be donated. Purging is hard work but immensely rewarding.

Identify Your Materials with Tags or Signage

Once you feel confident about the placement of your school-books and supplies, be sure to label as much as possible. Although I know where things go because I organized the area, my markings will increase the likelihood that it will stay orderly. A label maker or Post-it products greatly aid this goal. The bookshelves need labeling. Use a Sharpie to identify boxes and bags. Cute chalkboard tags are available nearly everywhere. When using baskets, use these tags to help you pinpoint their contents at a glance.

Paint Walls Bright Colors

Our schoolroom is painted a bright green and vibrant blue to coordinate with the world map that graces a whole wall. Paint your room yellow or bright white. Make it a happy space to spend your days in with your children.

Rotate Your Wall Maps and Posters

Coordinate with your studies for the year. I collect maps for each subject. The maps rotate based on our focus in a variety of subjects. Geography is a mainstay, but the science, English, and history posters rotate. Changing them out creates new interest. After a while, students stop examining the walls around them.

Learning Centers

As you finish organizing all the bigger categories in yours home-school space, think through areas that can be created to allow you to highlight one subject. This concept is super easy for younger students. Create a math manipulative station, a reading center, or a map area. Your imagination is the limit. Pinterest is full of excellent ideas. Generate some excitement for yours homeschool space.

Whiskers in one of his favorite spots

Prepare All Needed Supplies

You should have supply caddies, boxes, and extra sharp pencils. Dixon Ticonderoga wood-cased #2 pencils remain the best. This sounds silly to mention, but if you cannot appreciate the value of having a healthy stash of these excellent tools, stock up before you start each year. Locate a hole punch, stapler, and all other tools needed to make your job easy.

Purchase a wireless printer. This is a must for all homeschool moms. Once you have one in place, you'll wonder how you lived without it.

Think of what bothers you the most, and tackle that first. Once you figure out where you want to do school at your house and sort out your supplies, locate bookcases and storage containers. By grouping your books and supplies, your space works more efficiently. Painting your walls bright colors offers cheeriness and energy. Maps, learning centers, and supply boxes increase the productivity of any space.

Personally, I love finding organizing ideas for my homeschool space. Tomorrow is a new day. Try something new in your space.

CHAPTER 14

Summer

Don't let summer slip away. At our house, summers are usually purposely restful. We aim not to fill our summer with places to go and things to do that make us feel as though we are on a schedule. The school year dictates that we keep the schedule weekly. Summer offers promises of late-afternoon/early-evening lounging by the pool. In early April when we can hardly wait for summer to begin, the kids and I sit down and begin to plan on paper what we want our summer to involve. Sometimes we aim to work on a new skill. Some of the children in my house are working on music goals, such as learning to play the guitar and piano better. Scrapbooking and home-improvement projects are usually at the top of our list.

Early in the spring, I determine which books may be left over from the school year and which books we should read ahead to be prepared for the next semester. Reading makes up a significant part of our free time each summer. We look for reading contests that offer rewards for our hard work. Because of our diligence and insatiable interest in reading, some of my children have won first place in summer reading programs. Prizes have ranged from a fifty-dollar gift card to a collection of gift cards and have also included recognition, free food, and credit toward anything in the bookstore.

For all of us, summer promises time to spend with friends. Early in the summer, before the weather is too hot, we can venture to the zoo or a park. Play days with the children's friends include snacks and fun outings. I try to catch up with friends who don't cross my path regularly during the school year. I find it difficult during the school year to focus on projects around the house. My mind is occupied with school. Summer offers time for repairs and creative house projects.

Did I mention that summer also gives us long hours to complete cleaning-out projects and yard improvements? These might be no one's favorite choice of activities, the results are rewarding. Cleaning often unearths lost treasures and forgotten toys.

Although summer offers a vacation from schedules, be sure to use this block of time to meet your family's goals. Plan game or movie nights or cooking days along with those workdays.

CHAPTER 15

Keeping Your Home

Laundry

Why complicate a simple task? I'm not really sure why laundry seems to be a burden to so many. All I can relate to is how laundry works into our schedule. Tuesday is our first stay-at-home day of the week. So, early Tuesday morning after making coffee, I begin the laundry for the week. I usually start with the load of mixed-colored clothing. Each time the dryer stops, I try to respond immediately and fold all the clothes that were in it. I have a soft basket on top of the dryer that holds all clean socks. Along the wall, each child has a clean-clothes basket. The clothes coming out of the dryer are folded immediately and placed into the correct basket.

We have a laundry chute that comes down from the children's bathroom. One of the children is asked to change out the towels in the kids' bathroom and throw the dirty ones down the laundry chute. By sorting the clothes as soon as the dryer is finished, they never escape the laundry room. This habit has kept a stack of clean clothes begging to be folded from ever appearing in any other part of my house. It seems too much work to face several loads of laundry all at once. Think of the time required for folding several loads of laundry at one time. This is why so many moms are overburdened with a couch full of laundry waiting to be processed. Once laundry is complete for the week, I ask each child to promptly take his or her clean clothes up to his or her room and put them away.

Food

Due to the financial strain many families feel in the current economy, discussions about food costs occur more frequently than ever. In the last two years, I have been privileged to speak at numerous women's events saving money on groceries. Although I do use coupons to significantly lower my grocery costs, I titled my speech "Saving without Scissors." The following includes some of the ideas from my presentations.

When attempting to save money on food, families should assess how much they spend monthly on groceries. According to the USDA's 2012 report, a family of four spends somewhere between $629 and $1,250 on food monthly. This certainly represents a significant portion of your budget. What would you do if you had 50 percent of that money to spend monthly on other things? What motivates you to be a steward of the funds God has provided you?

Perhaps your family currently works hard to save money on food. I grew up helping my mother shop with $50 a week for a family of six. It seems that whether you are a family with small children or a mix of ages, costs for groceries and poultry items have been steadily climbing. Many rising costs offer us few options for keeping our spending in line with earnings. However, food is one of those more flexible categories. Perhaps you do most of the things that we are going to discuss. Congratulate yourself. As I have spoken to numerous women's groups, I have been stunned to discover that very few of these ideas are implemented in most homes. So, while I don't think they are profound, I put them here in print for you to peruse. Like most methods of saving, planning ahead is key.

Prepare, Plan, Stock Up, Save, Shop

Stock Basics—Pantry, Freezer, and Bathrooms

Whether you are in a new residence or you've kept house for years, do take stock of your pantry, freezer, and bathrooms. Some things in the pantry may need to be thrown out. Organize your pantry by categories. When you run out of something, immediately put it on your shopping list. For example, if you open your last bag of flour to refill your flour bin, write *flour* on your grocery list. This ongoing supply list will keep you from going back and forth to the grocery store during the week.

It might surprise you to know that I greatly dislike shopping, probably because I don't like spending money. When things are moving with the plan, I grocery shop significantly every two weeks, with a quick run for perishables during the week in between. Knowing what you need ahead of time assures you a more efficient system. Studies show that people who make frequent stops at the grocery store spend more money on food needs than those who shop once a week. So, do keep a list of your home and kitchen needs.

Look carefully into your pantry, freezer, and bathrooms for upcoming needs. Once you identify a list of items that are staples in your family, you will be able to look for these items at their best price and stock up until the sale occurs again. Bring items in your freezer forward so they don't spoil or become forgotten in the back. My husband spoiled me a few years ago by purchasing a full-size upright freezer. This makes organizing freezer foods so much easier. Meats are organized in the bottom of the freezer, with new purchases going toward the back. Although we don't hunt, we're blessed with four or five deer a year. When I pick up the deer meat from the processing plant, I work really hard to organize my freezer with items that need to be used first in front. We rarely throw out food. What's the point of saving money on food only to throw the food away? Although assessing your pantry, freezer, and bathroom storage takes a few minutes, the savings are worth it.

Develop a Meal Plan

If you intend to shop every two weeks, develop a two-week schedule of breakfasts, lunches, and suppers. Be flexible. With a little research, a myriad of options for planning two weeks of meals will be yours. One fun idea my sister implemented was to give every night of the week a theme. For example, Monday—Oriental; Tuesday—Mexican; Wednesday—Italian; Thursday—pizza; Friday—All-American; Saturday/Sunday—traditional.

Once you develop a plan, check your resources and build a grocery list based on the items you need to complete two weeks of meals. You might discover that your family is repeating the same meals every week or every other week. Aim to develop two menu plans. This gives you a month of planned meals. My guess is that you will have more variety in your family meals with this meal plan than you do currently.

Cook Your Food from Scratch

Making meals from fresh and raw ingredients saves enormously on your food costs. Think of purchasing food to make two pizzas for your family. At our house, this would cost about $7. Having pizza delivered costs between $20 and $25. Adding a salad or vegetable tray increases the nutritional value.

My youngest successfully completed his box garden last year. It yielded delicious fruit and vegetables. I am proud of him for reading about this project, troubleshooting, interviewing successful gardeners, and taking the project to completion. We look forward to more yummies.

Joseph's garden

Prepare More than One Meal at a Time

In other words, plan for two meals so that you will have leftovers. This gives some freedom on those busy days when you come home hungry without the time to prepare a meal. This might be on Sunday after church, when you have been at soccer practice, or when errands have kept you out later than expected. If you have an extra meal in the freezer or refrigerator, you might not be tempted to stop and purchase fast food for your family for $25 to $30.

If your family decides to cook in bulk, you might plan to prepare between four and ten meals at one time. Throughout my married life, one of my favorite books has been Emilie Barnes's *Once-a-Month Cooking*. The meal plans in this book are complete with recipes and shopping lists. Perhaps this will work for your family. My husband has very specific likes and dislikes in reference to food, so I picked through her suggestions, tried several new recipes, and built a plan based on her system.

Look through Refrigerator, Freezer, and Pantry to See What Needs to Be Used

When time allows, I straighten up these places before I shop so that unloading after shopping will be easier. When things are on schedule, I do the planning and straightening the day before I shop. Also check the bathrooms for items needed. They don't have consistent needs because toiletries are primarily nonperishable.

Shop Sale Cycles

Sales cycle around every three to six weeks. Once you know what items you use consistently in your home, you can search for them on sale. When they are at their lowest prices, stock up. This process requires alertness and work, but I have found that many of these items can easily be purchased in lots of twenty and thirty.

That way, I don't have to think about them for a while. Some items are marked down in a way that allows me to buy enough for six months.

Know Your Prices So You Can Evaluate Your Potential Savings

Watch carefully.

Bulk Cook and Freeze

Chicken, meatballs, cookie balls, lasagna, and calzones are just some of the foods that respond well to cooking ahead and freezing. Search online for bulk cooking. Once you discover what can be frozen, you will free yourself from a great deal of kitchen duty. Tackle these sorts of activities by making double what you need for a meal or setting aside a day to prepare meals for your freezer. On a busy day, the meals will be waiting on you. When you are committed to really focusing on school, you will be able to just select a meal and toss it in the oven. Once you add a fresh salad, you have a meal on the table effortlessly.

Flow with Seasons

Fresh fruits and veggies, soup: freeze excess in season. Don't be shy. I didn't grow up with a garden. I didn't know how to put anything up in the freezer from the garden. People who know these things are eager to share their knowledge. Find someone who knows, and ask her to teach you. As with all things unknown or hard, be a learner.

Buy in Bulk

Staples, beef, deer meat, grains, sugar, oats, and dry goods can be acquired in bulk. Save money by purchasing a twenty-five-pound bag of dry goods instead of a one-pound bag. This concept seems to be foreign to the audiences I have spoken to lately. Maybe it's old school. I like to think that I am nurturing my family by being prepared to feed them properly. Certainly, the boys who live at my house are greatly pleased with home-cooked and freshly fetched food. Just today, I sent an e-mail to my resource for bulk food requesting a twenty-five-to-fifty-pound bag of turbinado sugar. The popular idea that eating healthy costs more must be propagated by the makers of fake food. It simply is not true. It's a given that eating healthy forces a mom to be more prepared in order to acquire fresh food. Bulk-food options are available everywhere. Ask around or shop online for connection to your local resources. Some of the items we buy in bulk are oatmeal, raw sugar, wheat berries for making our own bread, lentils of all sorts, spices, and seasonal fruits and vegetables.

Focus on Five to Seven Sale Items at Each Store Each Week

Locate five to seven items on deep discount each week. Select only items that your family would buy anyway. Determine how many of each of the sale items your family needs for the next eight weeks. If you can purchase for the next six months, you will save more money and time.

Last year, when I was asked to do a story for our local TV station on couponing and saving on groceries, the reporter and cameraman accompanied me to Walgreens for my weekly shopping trip. The night before, the reporter and I had discussed how I was focusing on seven items that were deeply discounted that week. She expressed concern that we might have to shoot more footage on this story because this shopping trip would be small. I smiled. These items purchased in quantities of twenty would not be a small haul. If a family focuses on purchasing five items a week that are on deep discount, in six weeks they will have stockpiled thirty essential items at deeply discounted prices. Imagine the savings. Remember, only purchase items that you would normally use. Resist temptation and keep your goals in mind. Surprise does not even begin to describe the look on the reporter's face when I hauled two full baskets out of the store for less than twenty dollars. (Most of that twenty dollars was the tax on the items I was taking home.)

Not every week is successful. Sometimes there really isn't anything on sale that our family uses consistently. Have a plan. Work your plan. Enjoy the savings.

Limit Trips to the Grocery Store

Do big grocery runs two times monthly. If you create a food plan and the snacks are eaten too quickly, let everyone know that there won't be any more until it is time to shop again. Sometimes when I purchase an item on deep discount that is not on our normal list, people (I won't say who) think this means we can eat that food in bulk.

Summing Up Savings on Food

Make a list for a week or two from your food plan. Order coupons that fit items on sale. Clipboard the list for each store.

I rotate among Kroger, Walgreens, and Sam's Club. I might purchase other food items from bulk sources, fresh-food stands, and hunters.

Coupons

Take the weekly paper and look for an online source that lists the coupons. List sale items you need.

Shop eBay for that coupon from *Coupon Clipper*. Keep in mind that coupons add to your savings. However, simply shopping for an item's lowest price and purchasing it in bulk when it is the cheapest will ultimately have the largest effect on your budget. Most of the time when I use coupons, they are in conjunction with a sale, which takes 50 percent or more off the item's price. My approach with coupons is likely very different from that of most people. Like many, I have a large coupon binder. I have cut coupons, and I have bought extra papers so that I will have more coupons. When assessing the time and effort involved in saving with this approach, I was very disappointed.

Recently, I have simplified my approach. After determining which items I purchase regularly for my family, I take the weekly paper or look online and then compile a list of items on sale that week. Diligent people purchase newspapers in bulk and clip coupons. These compiled coupons are technically not for sale. But you may compensate clippers for their time and postage. Acquire coupons in bulk that match the savings at your store. If you reserve time to organize in this way, you can just shop the top sales of the week.

Ideally, I look at The Grocery Game on Sunday when the sale flyer for Walgreens has just been published. Walgreens is currently the best place to save money. After selecting the sale items for the week and printing my shopping list from The Grocery Game, I go to a clipping site and order my coupons in bulk. They usually arrive by Wednesday. We shop Friday or Saturday with clipboard, shopping list, and coupons. Simplicity is my game plan these days.

Other Helpful Sites

frugallysustainable.com

couponclippers.com

happymoneysaver.com

thebudgetdiet.com

livingrichlyonabudget.com

organizedhome.com

<u>Free Birthday Goodies</u>

heyitsfree.net/birthday-freebies

mrfreestuff.com/birthday-freebies

Free products may include toothbrushes, toothpaste, adhesive bandages, cough drops, deodorant, shampoo, razors, soap, laundry soap, lotion, shower gel, pain reliever, antacids, and more.

Contributions (Formerly Known as Chores)

All families function best when the work to maintain the home is evenly distributed. I have no illusion that, even with a well-laid-out schedule, the work at my house is accomplished efficiently. Resources are plentiful for methods of sharing daily and weekly tasks among all family members. Early on in my parenting, I heard a seasoned mom refer to chores as *contributions*. When I questioned her about this terminology, she shared that the semantics of *contributions* indicated that teamwork dominated in her home. The use of the word *chores* seemed to indicate that children were working for her instead of for themselves and with the team.

At our house, we intend to be dressed and ready for the day before we begin our academics. A determined plan does not indicate consistent success, but let me share some of our ideas.

On school mornings, children are asked to make their beds as soon as their feet hit the floor. Next comes brushing teeth, dressing, and eating breakfast. The next part of the schedule varies. Sometimes we gather for devotions and family time, which are followed by morning contributions. Other times, we complete contributions and then sit down to devotions. The second pattern is my favorite.

During the school year, morning contributions last from fifteen to twenty minutes. On many summer mornings, contributions take about an hour. For more ideas, look at the section on contributions appropriate for various ages. During our morning contributions, we feed the animals, give them fresh water, and brush them. We sweep the first floor, and we empty the dishwasher. The fourth helper's chores vary, taking into consideration urgent needs.

Weekly cleaning has occurred on Thursday for most of my parenting years. While I have tried a variety of schedules, the children are currently asked to contribute to family living space cleaning for an hour. They devote another hour to cleaning their rooms, which includes organizing dressers, straightening closets, cleaning under the beds, putting away clean clothes, putting away dirty clothes, hanging up the clothes on the floor, vacuuming their rooms, and dusting.

See the following for the cleaning schedule that is currently posted on our refrigerator.

Contributions for Team Simpson
Daily

Joseph - Pets, food, fresh water, pet :)

Josh - Vacuum 1st floor ALL

Mikayla - Dishwasher, Clean dishes in left sink

Katie - Check beds, bathrooms, mom's helper

Kitchen Cooking & Cleaning - Weekly

Day	Meals	Cleaning
Sun	Mom	Joseph
M	Joseph	Mom
T	Joseph	Joseph
W	Mikayla	Mikayla
Th	Mikayla	Mikayla
F	Josh	Josh
Sat	Katie	Josh

Thursday - Weekly (1 hour bedroom, 2 hours family contributions)

K - laundry, ironing, food prep & purchasing & cooking, pantry

M - downstairs bathroom & kid's bathroom, mop ALL 1st floor wood and tile, glass doors, litter box, fur on chairs

Josh - dust 1st floor, vac 2nd Floor, straighten & vac basement, shoe basket (sort & sweep), clean & vac 1 vehicle

Joseph - pantry/refrigerator, straighten garage, vac stairs, garbage-whole house, outside front door, sweep back steps

Learning housekeeping skills is essential for your children to become independent adults. Significant numbers of women in my generation entered marriage and parenting completely unequipped to manage their homes. Not long ago, I sat around the table with twelve like-minded moms following a brunch. The discussion about our mothers grew into a group therapy session. In this group of a dozen mothers, only two could claim that they felt properly prepared for the domestic tasks required in keeping a home. How shocking!

Although I always knew that I was gifted with an amazing mother, I was suddenly even more grateful for her. As I mentioned earlier, one summer, my mother assigned me the task of managing everything that related to keeping our house for an entire month. Although the task seemed daunting, I experienced a newfound confidence once I completed it. My domestic attempts were far from perfect. But my mother showed me how to correct my errors. By redoing jobs correctly, I moved closer to having usable skills.

About once a year, I take the time to train my children in new house skills. We usually rotate weekly jobs once a year. My experience suggests that I should demonstrate the correct procedure to complete a job and then supervise the job from the beginning numerous times. By talking it through while keeping my hands behind my back, my children learn to complete the job correctly. Perhaps you've heard the saying "Inspect what you expect." In this situation, I believe that my supervision of the job from beginning to end several times after demonstrating helps my child successfully master the skill. The expectations are clear. Correction is immediate. There's no need to wait for it to be checked. Certainly, a willing attitude increases the student's skill. Now that I have two very efficient teenage girls, I am assigning them the task of training their younger brothers in house jobs.

The kitchen continues to house a constant flow of activity. One might imagine that the kitchen would be busy with meal preparation and cleanup. Some of those who reside at my house, however, view the kitchen as open for activity all hours of the day. While I don't want anyone to go hungry at my house, I really desire to see the kitchen clean periodically. Frequently, visitors to the kitchen make a snack but fail to clean up after themselves.

Teaching your children to cook and clean the kitchen is of utmost importance. From a practical standpoint, all adults will need to cook and clean the kitchen. When my girls babysit, they check to make sure that the kitchen is completely clean with wiped counters. Contributing to the maintenance of the kitchen is an invaluable skill for my boys to master as well. They benefit from the activities in the kitchen; they should learn how to properly clean the kitchen. Although they are young, they have already seen how cleaning the kitchen at a friend's house earned them points with the friend's mom. Domestic skills have sometimes been divided between males and females. For example, many believe that only males should take out the trash and mow the grass. They promote the concept that only women should cook and clean inside the house. My contention is that all jobs should be learned by all. Think of domestic responsibilities as team activities.

Changing clothes out for seasons requires diligence and some level of organization. In late fall, we transition to winter clothes. In early spring, we sort through winter. Since this is a family-size job, we strategize on the best way to complete the work. Usually, we begin with the youngest children. My younger four were born in five years. It seems that they came in pairs. The youngest two are just eighteen months apart. In a similar pattern, the girls are just eighteen months apart. So, I begin with the younger two.

Initially, we go through all the drawers and closets. Clothes that are too small are put into the "sell" or "give-away" stack. If they fit but are too warm to keep out, they are placed in a box with the size marked on the outside. Once space is prepared in the closets and drawers, we look through stored boxes for clothes from last season and clothes that were too big that were bought ahead or from consignment. The clothes are organized in groups on the floor along the wall. Brightly colored three-by-five cards in front of the stacks identify the piles. Once we know what we have for the new season, we arrange them neatly in drawers and the closet. This process includes a great deal of trying on of clothes. The size marked in any garment can be misleading. As a side note, this is a great time to count all personal items and throw out items that are too small or just worn out. Replacement of these items feels good.

Sorting through the girls' area goes much the same. Sharing our smaller items with those who need them feels great. Some of the items are put back for resale, but more than half of them are shared with friends or our local Sudanese community. (We love to share with our international friends. One ministry that we undergird is the settling of Sudanese refugees to this country. Many of the lost boys of Sudan have found their way here. It blesses my heart to share.)

Determine where to start with your "need" list after sorting through what you already have put back from last year and bought ahead. All our stored clothes are packed away in boxes and marked, for example, "boy, size 10" or "girl, size 4." Many of our clothes come from consignment sales. Hand-me-down bags are some of our favorite sources. In return, we love to share the clothes that we have outgrown. Rarely is the giver of shared clothes the same person with whom we share our hand-me-downs. This generosity is a joy to receive but even better to bestow. It would consume at least a chapter to tell how we collect and process clothes for each of us. When the children were younger and I had to do most of the clothes transfer by myself, I would start with the youngest two and work my way up. Over the years, people have been very kind to us in sharing outgrown clothing. We in turn have gifted cousins, friends, and some of our Sudanese friends from church.

Everyone must develop her own pattern. We start with shoes and fringe items such as coats, gloves, and socks. We determine which items are too small, missing half a pair, or simply out of season. Sports shoes and paraphernalia seem to consistently land in high-traffic areas when they should be stored for the next season.

Next, we sort each dresser drawer. All seasonal clothes go in one of three piles: "donate" or "save for next season" or "keep in the drawers." Since we currently live in a moderate climate, some pants and all shirts with short sleeves are kept in the drawers almost year-round.

Once the dressers are almost empty and ready for the new season, work on the closets begins. The same routine applies here. What clothes are too small? Which ones need to be shared? And which ones stay? The working closets consist primarily of dress and Sunday-related attire, with some dress-up items and jackets. Once all is sorted, we complete the activity by loading the van with things to donate. We store items for later in plastic storage bins and giant Ziploc bags and reestablish order in drawers and closets.

In my family, I sort the two younger boys' areas. Then I work with both the girls at the same time. Finally, I sort my oldest son's clothing. Now that he's in college, I am mainly dealing with the younger four. In reality, the girls are doing most of their own season changes. Since both of them are nearly finished growing, less change is necessary. Twice a year, when we change clothes in our rooms, we assess personal items. It seems that socks always pose desperate needs. How mysteriously socks behave! So many extras exist. Periodically, all odd socks must be thrown away. This activity is very liberating. Create a list of all socks, personal items, shoes, pants, shirts, dresses, and other items needed.

Clothes that are too big but were purchased for a deal, consignment finds, and clothes that won't be worn until next season are stored in file boxes. Once the remaining items are sorted by gender and size, they are stashed on the top shelves in the children's closets. Just recently, we began storing some seasonal clothing in our attic. Although the summers are hot where we live, the clothes seem to be just fine. Select a system that works for you based on your climate, number of kids, and storage space.

Numerous friends have asked me about how I store clothes. As you become a mother and are responsible for many wardrobes, storage and organization become serious topics. Early in my married life, I read all of Emilie Barnes's books on organization. One of the many concepts that has stayed with me all these years is the idea of buying matching-size boxes for storage. For nearly twenty years, I have stored clothing, crafts, Christmas items, seasonal and holiday items, and a myriad of other items in white file boxes. Recently I have become determined to change most of the paper boxes in the attic to plastic storage bins. Cooler weather seems to be the best time to reorganize the attic. When transferring items, I find that donating and throwing away bring even more space to the storage location.

When Should I Seasonally Clean?

Seasonal cleaning and sorting must be accomplished with a schedule that best fits your family. While I aim to straighten and clean out all spaces in my home once a year, some areas are still neglected. All mothers face the challenges of scrambling to keep everything clean at the very same time.

When you're feeling concerned about keeping everything straightened up, remember that you live in your home. A sign that used to hang in my garage entrance read, "The house was clean yesterday, sorry you missed it." An expression that my husband enjoys repeating is "If you're coming to see the house, call ahead. If you're coming to see us, come on." An excellent quote that I read recently states, "I am not aiming for perfection, just excellence." For me, these ideas apply to cleaning as much as to anything. My primary goal is to be hospitable. Although my personality screams organization before relaxation and fun, I aim to let that standard go so that I can enjoy my family and those who come to visit. Once we complete our cleaning with our best effort, we relax and enjoy time together.

My children love to finish school early so that we can do a cleaning project. That probably sounds strange to many people. At the beginning of most breaks, such as Christmas, spring, and summer, we tackle a list of maintenance cleaning projects. This might involve cleaning out a closet, the pantry, the garage, the attic, or the flower beds. Often, we take a day or two and designate them for cleaning or bulk cooking. My family is used to this routine and seems to easily cooperate. As the kids have grown older, I have begun to break them into teams that will function efficiently. For example, now that I have two boys and two girls at home, I put one boy with one sister to tackle a task. Sometimes I write the cleaning activities for the day on different pages or small dry-erase boards. The task sheet or board is then assigned to a team or individual. Ideally, tasks are checked off and approved as completed. Once again, explaining this subject could consume a chapter.

CHAPTER 16

Taking Care of Yourself

Skydiving...just because

As I am writing this chapter, we are enjoying the month of May. As you have read in this book, intentionality dominates as a theme. I am intentional about work, but I aspire to be just as intentional about play. Some who know me well may find this humorous. Just as work is more productive when planned, however, play is also more fun when planned.

Quiet time is a necessity. The older I get, the more I feel my work is never done. Strangely, the older my children become, the more work there seems to be. So, in order to function at my optimal level, I must plan for revitalization. You know yourself. What refreshes you? Plan for daily, weekly, and periodic recharging. The perfect cup of coffee in the morning is part of my routine. If I wake up too early in the morning, I spend time quietly talking to God about my concerns for the day ahead. I pray that I will know His intention for my day. Often, I am overwhelmed by the number of seemingly urgent things that need to be done in a given day. Clearly, this type of schedule would not be God's plan for my day. I ask God for wisdom. My husband is a great sounding board for making decisions. Sometimes the number of open tabs on my computer indicates the busyness of my mind. Keeping a thought toward the big picture often clarifies my decisions.

Quiet rest is relevant to a healthy, productive, and godly life. Although I need only about seven hours of sleep, I aim for eight hours. Going to bed at a reasonable time is imperative. Lack of sleep ages my body, makes for a grouchy mom, and does not allow me to function at my optimal level.

My girls compete in speech and debate tournaments. During these competitions, it is impossible to sleep more than about six hours a night. When we get home, I schedule a day to unpack, rest, and recuperate. Before any trip, we usually clean the house. Returning to a clean house eliminates much of the pressure of reentry. Reentering the schedule at home with fatigue prohibits success and results in mistakes.

Many books have been written on sleep and fatigue. The hardest thing for me is going to bed on time. The night hours are so quiet and appealing. When I am not interrupted, I work at high speed. Leisurely activities in those silent hours are bliss. So, the temptation to stay up very late is always with me. My bedtime is really between 11:00 p.m. and midnight. In order to read before bed, I head to my room about 10:00 p.m. If I don't stay with this plan, either my reading or my bedtime is sabotaged. When this is the case, I forgive myself and try again the next night with more resolve.

Be good to yourself. A dear friend said this to me when my children were very young, and I often repeat it to myself. While many do a great job keeping up with their personal needs, I would suspect that most of the moms reading this book need encouragement to take care of themselves. Most of the best moms I know take care of everyone else before they take care of themselves.

In keeping with this goal of better self-care, I plan for an afternoon out as we finish each school year. At this intersection, I treat myself to a one-hour massage. If you do this at another time of year, you could call it a teacher in-service. Any self-care needs no excuse, only a funny name. My own mother has youthfulness about her. She emphasizes skin care and drinking lots of water. Moisture on my skin is a critical need. At all ages, women need to nurture their skin. This topic could fill its own book.

While I don't fall into the group of moms who emphasize their needs over those of their children, I do believe that caring for yourself allows you to care properly for your children. Let's face it: as humans, we are innately selfish. Test yourself. When your husband calls or comes home, do you immediately ask him how he is doing or how his day was? Or do you want to tell him all about your day or something that you need him to do?

Teaching your children to work diligently in addition to training them to replenish themselves is invaluable. Do they work hard and play hard? Do they work hard but not rest or eat properly? Or do they play too much? Balance is such a tricky thing. Balance must be the goal every time we assess our commitments and schedules. If my life is out of sync, how can I set an example of balance for my children? What a sobering thought. Revisit your overall schedule at least three times a year. Question whether you are in balance physically, mentally, and spiritually. I often start with the question of physical health when I am reassessing. Am I rested?

This question of rest brings us to the next thought about assessing your schedule. As you complete the school year, consider creating time for the activities you enjoy most. Ask your children to do the same. When I began to ask what they would enjoy doing over the summer, they never struggled to give me ideas. I actually write them down. Once I've gathered suggestions, I make plans to have friends over, to go on field trips, and to do other learning activities. Overall, planning to rest or do more fun activities ensures that we don't just float through our days without purpose. Resting well counts as intentionality.

So, what are some of my favorite relaxing activities?

- Reading a book for pleasure…not for school preparation

- Swinging in my ENO

- Decorating my home

- Taking a long bath

- An hour-long massage at a spa

- Lunch or coffee with a friend

- More time for yoga or Pilates

- Trying a new recipe with fresh, in-season foods

One of my favorite things to do...Sing and play my guitar

Resting in the Summer

Some of the activities we plan for the summer are swimming, reading, and having friends over. Our summer day usually involves cognitive activities and cleaning in the morning hours. Early afternoon is reading time. After three, we head out for swimming and activities outdoors. Since we live in the Deep South, it is very hot in the summer. Two of my children burn quickly. The rest of us really do not need sunburns either. If we miss the middle of the day in the sun, we don't burn or need sunscreen. As expected, pool visits necessitate a cooler of drinks and fun food. All the kids know how to pack a fabulous cooler. Teaching children of all ages to make sandwiches in bulk comes in handy. Packing a cooler for dinner saves serious money. Long, lazy hours by the pool are often rewarded with conversations with my children or a friend.

Summer offers the best time to spend hours playing with friends. Early in the summer, we can enjoy a day at the zoo, the botanical gardens, or a favorite park. It's challenging to schedule long play days for the children during the school year. Summer days are great for lazy play. We can invite friends who attend traditional school over during this time. The girls plan overnights for watching movies and eating mounds of ice cream and popcorn. Did I mention chocolate? Planning a day or half a day out with each child separately is also one of my favorite things to do during the summer months.

Another dominant activity in this period of summer rest is deep cleaning. During the school year and even over Christmas break, spending a day or half a day cleaning through a closet or room would be impossible. Breaks between semesters and over the summer, however, allow more time for cleaning projects. On an enthusiastic note, cleaning usually means finding lost treasures and acquiring additional space. Improvements might dictate purchasing things such as a new rug, organizing containers, or new bedding. Generally, we find our home to be more pleasant once we complete deep cleaning.

Somewhat mysteriously to me, the spaces that I cleaned through last year become cluttered and crowded again. This situation necessitates yearly cleaning in all spaces. A clean and organized space actually makes Mom and family feel more relaxed. The difficult work of decision-making while cleaning proves worth the effort. Some struggle with keeping things that might be useful in the future. When I was growing up, my family had limited funds, so repurposing was vital. If you are prone to using things until they are completely unusable, sorting and decluttering might prove more challenging. Recruit an organizer in your family or among your friends to assist you. Refer to chapter 15 for further ideas on maintaining your home.

Happy Husband—Go on Dates, Make Lunches, Keep Company

US

Remember when a date with your husband, previously your boyfriend, was the highlight of your day or week? Spend time remembering how you planned every detail of those experiences. Do you remember thinking through your outfit, making sure that you smelled and looked great, and preparing for success? Think of time with your husband as a treat for both of you. Recently, a dear friend of mine gave me chocolate, dark chocolate, as a birthday present. As you might imagine, I hid the chocolate so that I could enjoy it slowly. Purposely, I rewarded myself with one small square of chocolate from time to time. Truthfully, sometimes it was three squares of chocolate. Just as I look forward to setting aside time to savor that dark chocolate, I look forward to time early in the morning and late at night in conversation with my husband. Often in the early morning, we have long conversations, playtime, and a perfect cup of coffee. Late at night, we talk through the day, read scripture, journal, watch the news, and enjoy each other's company.

In Kona, Hawaii

When planning time alone, think of dates at home and out. My children are now old enough to stay home by themselves. This provides us the freedom to go out to dinner and talk without interruption. If I turn my phone off and we can be reached only on Dad's phone, the children rarely call. *The Entertainment Book* is full of buy-one-get-one-free (BOGO) dinners. Groupon and Living Social offer other deals on meals. Dinner at a fine restaurant is an occasional treat, but a sandwich at Chick-fil-A or a shared meal at On the Border is perfect too. The goal is to enjoy each other's company.

Without going into detail, prioritizing alone time with your husband improves your day as well as his. Think of it this way: God created a beautiful thing when He created intimacy within marriage. This is the glue. This is the magic. This is fun. Prioritize alone time by putting the children to bed early with an audiobook, lighting candles in your bedroom, and selecting a movie ahead of time. Buy his favorite snack. Order a new outfit just for his viewing. Keep the conversation positive. Treasure the opportunity to enjoy marriage. Plan a date night at home or out at least once a week.

Here are a few pictures of my handsome husband.

Tim visiting the volcano on the Big Island of Hawaii

Tim as a pilot – one of his favorite things to do

One last thought about taking care of yourself: Remember that, in addition to being a wife and mother, you are also likely a daughter, sister, and aunt. Be purposeful in these roles too. Perhaps your mother is far away like mine is. Write, call, and visit. Be the daughter you want your daughter to be to you. Some mothers are a joy. Others are not. Navigate each relationship with the plan to finish well.

My mother is great fun. Through the years, she has been a great conversationalist. We share so much. When I was younger, she taught me how to study my Bible, to teach children Bible stories, to sing worship music, to complete a list of domestic chores, and to be generous. My dad gives the best hugs and is always eager to catch up on all the news. The older I get, the more time I want to spend with them.

My sister and I plan lunch and shopping. With nine children between us, we mastered planning park days and field trips. If you think about it, we make eleven without asking anyone else. At many places, we qualify for the group discount with ten. Take your role as aunt seriously too. Do what you can to be fun. Be attentive when in conversations. Plan outings, and don't forget birthdays.

Overall, when you take care of yourself, you will be better equipped to take care of others. *Others* can mean your immediate family or your extended family. Be good to yourself so that you can be good to those you love.

For all of my beach-loving friends, I wish I could share a picture of my most favorite beach in the world, Hapuna. This beach is on the Kona side of the Big Island, where I grew up. Imagine your favorite beach. Take a moment and close your eyes to feel the warm sand between your toes. Smell the salty breeze. Feast your eyes on this glimpse of heaven.

As often as possible, pause and breathe deeply.

CHAPTER 17

Contributing Financially

Homeschooling and raising children require more energy than a body can muster on most good days. Yet there is also housekeeping, food fetching, and meal preparing, not to mention the needs of your husband calling for your attention daily. I am compelled to mention, however, that, when possible, we need to be like the woman in Proverbs 31 who contributes to the financial benefit of her home. Certainly, we can contribute financially by saving money in the way we plan meals and cutting costs for food and clothing. Whenever possible, it is prudent to search for ways to barter or work in exchange for your family's needs.

When my husband and I were first married, we did not spend any of the money that I made. I worked outside the home for nearly seven years before we had children. Those funds were immediately put into savings. Initially, we saved for a home we intended to buy. Once we bought our first lot and built our first home, we put money away for other goals. My husband's income paid the bills and met our budget plans. Any financial gain I made once we had children paid for their clothing, music lessons, classes out, and homeschool supplies. Assess your skill set and determine how you might be able to contribute to the financial costs of your home.

Some of my friends are trained nurses. There are always part-time jobs available for those in medical fields. Another very marketable skill for stay-at-home moms is teaching piano or, really, any musical instrument. Some moms clean houses, work weekends, or create a product from home. The ideas are endless. Do what you love. Think hard about what is needed in the area in which you live. With so much business being done via the Internet on sites like Instagram and Etsy, there is no limit to what you can pursue. As you come up with ideas, ask others for their input. Be teachable by really listening to their responses. The more brains that think through marketable ideas, the more successful your efforts will be once you launch them.

About halfway through our homeschooling journey, I realized that I desperately needed help grading. With so many children, I also needed help with some one-on-one instruction. God gave me Miss Patti, who refused to take any payment. She claims that she needs all the deposits she can make in her heaven bank. For all the days she spent grading, teaching handwriting, giving spelling tests (Imagine giving and grading five spelling tests every week!), tagging along on field trips, and just jumping in where needed, *thank you!*

Your rewards are eternal.

Miss Patti

One mother I knew desperately wanted braces for her children. She spoke to the selected orthodontist, asking if there was anything that she could do for him in his office or his home in exchange for braces for her children. As a result, she cleaned his office for the agreed-on amount of time in exchange for her children's braces. Both parties were very pleased with the exchange.

Another creative mother painted five rooms in someone's home in exchange for the use of the person's beach house for a week. Her family could not have afforded a vacation without this exchange. Bartering always presents exciting options. My husband is an excessively talented man who never ceases to amaze me. His impressive recording voice has served to barter for glasses for the family, professional photos, and numerous other items. Everyone has skills and talents. Do what you know you do well. Think through the market options, and work your plan.

Suppose you want music lessons for your children, but the cost of the lessons is out of your range. Consider offering to clean house for the music teacher in exchange for lessons. Really, be creative. Do you need a pressure washer to clean something at your house? Presuming you don't own one, perhaps someone who does would be willing to let you clean her patio with her pressure washer in exchange for its use at your place. Maybe you've been dreaming of having date nights with your husband more often. Think hard. Maybe you know of a friend with the same desire. Could you switch babysitting nights so that each of you could have a night out without the cost of a babysitter? Or do you have the gift of photography? Could you photograph an important event in exchange for something that your family needs? The examples are endless.

Be creative. Be prepared to work hard. Always give more than you think the other party expects from the barter.

Don't be discouraged. Think of a solution. Assess your gifts. Pray for wisdom.

CHAPTER 18

Books—a Scholarly Home

Charlotte Mason said, "education is an atmosphere, a discipline, and a life,"[7] and she was right. An extensive study published in 2010 in *Family Scholarly Culture and Educational Success* reports that a family's "scholarly culture—the way of life in homes where books are numerous, esteemed, read, and enjoyed" matters.[8] Many of the ideas in this chapter were gleaned from an article by Janice Campbell called "Taking Time for Things That Matter."

I'm sure this doesn't come as a surprise to homeschoolers, but just in case you need a reason to keep building your family's home library, here are a few significant quotes from the report.

A home in which books are an integral part of the way of life will encourage children to read for pleasure, thereby providing them with information, vocabulary, imaginative richness, and wide horizons.[9]

Because it generates skills and knowledge central to schooling, scholarly culture should enhance educational achievement in all societies, rich and poor alike; in all political systems, Communist and capitalist alike; and in the past as well as the present.

In addition to providing skills and knowledge, a large home library is a manifestation of the family's preferences: an indication that they enjoy and value scholarly culture, that they find ideas congenial, reading agreeable, complex and intellectually demanding work attractive. It shows a commitment to investing in knowledge, and perhaps in schooling. It suggests that conversations between parents and their children will include references to books and imaginative ideas growing out of them. In short, a large library reveals a preference for the scholarly culture.[10]

Whiskers doing school (or keeping us from doing school)

Biggest gains at the bottom: an increase in scholarly culture has the greatest impact on children from families with little scholarly culture.

Each additional book is associated with greater gains in educational attainment in families with few books than in families where there are already many books.

The difference between a bookless home and one with a five-hundred-book library is as great as the difference between having parents who are barely literate (three years of education) and having university-educated parents (fifteen or sixteen years of education).

Scholarly culture's advantage goes back for generations, as far back as the memory of survey respondents can take us, and in all political systems (both pre- and post-WW II West, pre- and post-Communist Eastern Europe, pre– and post–Cultural Revolution China, and pre- and post-Apartheid South Africa).[11]

Thus it seems that scholarly culture, and the taste for books that it brings, flows from generation to generation largely of its own accord, little affected by education, occupational status, or other aspects of class.[12]

Parents give their infants toy books to play with in the bath; read stories to little children at bedtime; give books as presents to older children; talk, explain, imagine, fantasize, and play with words unceasingly. Their children get a taste for all this, learn the words, master the skills, and buy the books. And that pays off handsomely in school.

A book-oriented home environment, we argue, endows children with tools that are directly useful in learning at school: vocabulary, information, comprehension skills, imagination, broad horizons of history and geography, familiarity with good writing, understanding of the importance of evidence in argument, and many others. In short, families matter not just for the material resources they provide, not just because of parents' formal educational skills, but also—often more importantly—because of the scholarly culture they embody.[13]

Another article by Janice Campbell that you may enjoy is called "How to Build a Quality Home Library Inexpensively."[14]

> Books are not made for furniture,
> but there is nothing else that so
> beautifully furnishes a house.
> —HENRY WARD BEECHER

> Books are the compasses and telescopes
> and sextants and charts which other
> men have prepared to help us navigate
> the dangerous seas of human life.
> —JESSE LEE BENNETT

The stories of childhood leave an indelible
impression, and their author always has a niche
in the temple of memory from which the image
is never cast out to be thrown on the rubbish
heap of things that are outgrown and outlived.
—HOWARD PYLE

Scholarly pursuits are not the easy route. Living purposefully with
your time creates satisfying habits. Consider the environment that
reading books generates in your home. Be intentional.

CHAPTER 19

Nurturing Your Home

urturing implies cultivating. When you desire a strong home, a consistent boost of love and care coupled with intentional actions brings healthy results. Entire libraries have been written to speak to the home and family, but this chapter includes just a few key ideas to incorporate.

Determining what and when for family is actually what makes each family's times uniquely theirs. Some families love outdoor activities, such as camping and boating. Others love road trips. (This one is ours, for sure.) Cooking and doing projects together bonds families in fun. The range is unlimited as it relates to the imagination.

Reading Time

Whether you are homeschooling or not, reading time enriches in so many ways. Since we are homeschooling, the schedule is bent toward reading time in the afternoon. As previously noted, we complete core academics in the morning. Afternoons (after 2:00 p.m.) are devoted to reading time, followed by projects and housecleaning.

We select reading material from history, biographies, literature, science, and selected excellent reads. For homeschool students, lists for primary reading and read alouds offer outstanding selections, and those books can be incorporated into school requirements. Schedule time to complete these assignments. For traditional school students, purposeful reading selections ensure the guided development of the mind. Leaving reading to random selection confirms that your child's mind will be developed by those who select the books for the library or local bookstore. Purposeful reading elevates the mind.

Since reading is heavenly to some and distasteful to others, creating an appealing environment draws in the more reluctant. One of our ploys for pleasant reading is a basket of cozy blankets. Tasty snacks saved just for reading time divert reluctant participants. Our favorites include warm chocolate cookies. Actually, any warm cookies will do. Popcorn, trail mix, puppy chow (especially with Nutella), chips, licorice, M&Ms, and fresh homemade bread with homemade jelly are a few of our regular choices.

Location plays a key part in success. We love to read in our living room, where everyone has a great seat. For afternoon reading, this is perfect. Another place for awesome reading is the van. No kidding! Think of how practical this is for families. Some days we drive quite a bit. Audiobooks or a designated reader accomplishes a delightful activity of scholarly time. Our family has clocked countless hours on the road while involved in sports and forensic competition. Some might just chill and have free time when they travel around town or out of town, but being intentional with these blocks of time is quite rewarding in developing the whole child.

When working through the challenging time of reading versus social media or watching a video, determine that school hours are used for school activities: a purpose to develop versus just passing the time. Keep in mind that relaxation is virtuous if it is earned with hard work. As with so many things in life, balance is key.

Returning to the idea of reading time in the living room at home, activities that occupy the hands while listening actually generate a substantially greater absorption of the material heard. Some of my kids are very wiggly. Certainly, all homes with little people have wiggles. Keeping their hands busy with a box or tray of Legos, jewelry-making items, crochet and knitting projects, model building, or K'NEX allows their minds optimal digestion of the reading material. Other ideas include sorting and folding socks, ironing, mending, cleaning small items, sorting drawers, and other various domestic activities. Sometimes we keep boxes under the couches for each listener. This allows for ongoing activities to be readily available.

Individual reading comes easily for eager readers. Setting aside time for reading helps all to be successful. Designated time for nonreaders ensures that it happens. As mentioned before, select your child's reading. This book includes suggested book lists that optimize the development of any child. Summers offer long stretches of time that can be designated for reading. As indicated throughout this book, if we don't plan purposefully, our time will just evaporate. This is not a unique concept. See chapter 18 for more information on a scholarly home.

Game Night

Game night is a brilliant way to build teamwork and make memories within a family. Families who do this well often select Friday or Saturday night for hours of fun. Incorporate game night when your children are as young as possible. If kids learn to win and lose gracefully at a young age, they have gained an immensely valuable tool.

One mother told me she would never do game nights because her children would fight. It would never work at her house because her kids didn't get along. In this case, game nights might be *more* important, so the kids learn to get along with one another and with others. Selfishness and pride might be dominating their responses. Do they not expect to ever lose? Do they not know how to cheer for others when they are losing? Do they realize that much of life is how the dice rolls when there is nothing they can do to affect the situation? Imagine the character gained while practicing the correct responses to winning as well as losing, cheering others on, dealing with disappointment while finishing the game, not gloating when winning, and just learning how to have fun. Thinking of the long-term value of game nights creates a new energy to ensure that they happen.

Road Trips

Simpsons all carry and operate cameras

Since much of what makes families wonderful are happy memories, road trips must be high on the list when nurturing our homes. Road trips can be elaborate and take months of planning. Driving may take a few hours or days. The trip may cost a small amount or a considerable fortune. It may be the trip of a lifetime or a yearly road trip. Consider your goals and your resources.

Take lots of pictures. Plan fun food. Include your kids' ideas. Planning can be half the fun. The anticipation of a trip is certainly a pleasurable activity at our house. Staying within budget is a high priority. Necessary choices need to be made before leaving.

Decide how much to spend each day on food. Consider eating in your room or camper, or simply bring a cooler. If you save on some of the day's food, your budget may allow for a splurge in other areas. Perhaps you'll decide to spend on activities and keep the food light. Each situation will be different. Saving for a vacation so you can pay as you go eliminates the not-so-much-fun part of paying off the credit-card bill from a trip. Don't do things backward.

This list of nurturing ideas briefly touches on ways to build your family. Think through the distinct characteristics of your family. Devise plans for activities that shape your relationships.

CHAPTER 20

Ten Ways to Save Money on Homeschooling

Whether you are just beginning your homeschool journey or are somewhere down the road, the cost of homeschooling is not a small concern. On this twenty-year journey, I have found ways to save. Discover new ways to eliminate costs in one or more of these ten ways to save money on homeschooling.

Most homeschool moms need to find ways to save money. Although we pay for public education with our tax dollars, our choice to homeschool means that we pay again for our children's education. Between curriculum, furniture, field trips, homeschool group costs, and a myriad of other expenses, saving money is a necessity. Although ideas on how to spend money are everywhere, what follows is a list of ten ways to save money on homeschool costs. Let's flesh out some of these ideas. Saving money is easy.

1. <u>Make a list of all items you need before buying any-thing.</u> It is really dangerous to go shopping without a list. Without direction, shoppers usually come home with more than they need. Most of us have experienced this risk in other situations, such as when we drop by the grocery store without a list when we are hungry. Shopping for curriculum is much the same and equally dangerous. List all the books and supplies you need. Aimlessness will cost you extra money.

2. <u>Shop used bookstores, Amazon, eBay, local book sales, and Facebook resale groups.</u> Used homeschool books are also available online. Once your list for the school year is complete, start by identifying the price of each item. Watch for the edition of each of the books you need. If your student is taking a tutorial class or you are teaching a group, be sure that the editions of your books match. This avoids unnecessary frustration. If you are schooling multiple kids, you might want to keep the answer key from an older child's book and just buy the workbook. Be sure you purchase the answer key whenever it is available. Saving time with an answer key is always a smart plan.

Currently, the local used-book sale is my first stop for books. Deals are everywhere. Knowing what I need and the original price allows me to negotiate or select the best price. Nearly new or new books sell for 50 to 75 percent off their original price. More-used books or resources often sell for a fraction of their original price.

My second place to hunt is Amazon or eBay. With Amazon Prime, shopping for books has never been easier. Keep an eye on the location of the seller, the shipping time, and the postage price. Often, there is a hidden cost in the shipping that eliminates the value of one item over another. Although eBay offers another location for books, the sorting process on Amazon greatly speeds up the process for me.

Another new but reliable source for the items on your list is Facebook resale groups. One advantage of these is that they offer large items such as bookshelves, chairs, and tables locally. The search box gives a quick collection of all items in a needed category. If you fail to locate what you need, simply place an "in search of" (ISO) post identifying your need.

Finally, online homeschool sites are best located by referrals. Don't forget that the sites that offer great deals for purchases are also excellent for selling your used resources. Cleaning out at the end of every school year is as important as planning ahead for the next year. Decide what source is best for your needs. Buying used always saves money.

3. <u>Buy collapsible tables and chairs—they are multipurpose and allow you to change configuration.</u> Selecting flexible furniture for your homeschool space allows you to rearrange it each semester or year. This brightens the mood. Chairs and tables can be folded up for breaks. Our school space doubles as a ping-pong and sleepover space for large groups.

These folding furniture pieces often come in handy when doing a garage sale, selling at a craft fair, or just doing some expanded entertaining. When hosting parties, you can use these tables to hold the drinks, food, or displays. Our parties vary in location from outside on the patio to inside the house. Adaptable pieces provide wonderful options.

My favorite pieces include the four-foot tables, six-foot tables, and comfortable folding chairs. Changing the arrangement of these tables allows variety without a new cost. The kids love to come into a new month, new semester, or new year with a fresh grouping.

In the kitchen – one of my favorite places to be

4. <u>Save money by cooking meals at home rather than eating out.</u> Although this habit is difficult to implement, the savings of eating out of a cooler motivates even a reluctant parent. For many years, we counted how many sandwiches we needed for the week. Sandwiches assembled on Sunday afternoon were packaged into individual

bags. Chips, cookies, fruit, trail mixes, and applesauce were loaded into the snack drawers, ready for the next day. Some years, we packed individual lunch boxes. Other years, we compiled a family cooler for the week.

We ate these meals on road trips, at soccer games, at tournaments, on field trips, and whenever we were planning to be out at mealtime. Occasionally, we would decide to pick up fast food. This worked if we located a Chick-fil-A, but disappointment would set in at almost any other option. The boys developed the attitude that eating out of the cooler would provide more food. This was true. Another advantage was that we could eat whenever we were hungry instead of hunting for food. Ultimately, we cut our food costs in half by eating out of a cooler. So for combining convenience, more food, and savings, the cooler option is the winning plan.

5. <u>Trade teaching or other skills.</u> Exchange of goods and services is traditional business. Why not apply practical business ideas to homeschooling? Teach to your strengths, and trade out for what you need. Trade skills instead of money.

What do I mean by this? Let's say that your gifts lie in the area of English. Perhaps you are weak in math. Ideally, locate someone with math aptitude whose child needs tutoring in English. Offer an exchange of services that seems equitable. Always aim to create a swap in which the other person feels he received more in the exchange.

If you cannot find such an easy swap, trade a service such as housecleaning, gardening, yard work, painting, babysitting, mulching and weeding flower beds, sewing, music lessons, repairs, or a variety of other abilities. Pray about your child's needs. Ask God for creative thoughts.

Sometimes a direct trade does not work, but you can do some extra work to pay for the tutoring or class your child needs to be successful. Remember, it is only a season. Your perseverance and hard work will bring a hefty reward.

6. <u>Use the library rather than buying books new.</u> Once again, a carefully assembled list of the books you need will allow time for you to call ahead. We love to read books from Veritas Press and Sonlight lists. Granted, we purchase most of our books used or new, but sometimes the library offers an additional place to gather reading materials. Summers and breaks allow us to read intentionally too.

Our library system cheerfully allows calls requesting any books. Calling ahead allows the librarian to pull the books or order them from another branch. Once all the desired books are waiting for us at the librarian's desk, we drop by and check them out. This saves an immense amount of time. Instead of searching for every book in the library or traveling to a library that is not ours, we just order the books from our list. Seriously, this is good stuff.

7. <u>Don't buy everything unless you need it.</u> One easy mistake to make when ordering curriculum involves ordering too much. Many companies that we use for core subjects sell to private and public schools as well. Consider that they provide sources geared toward classroom environments. Although these lesson plans and game ideas work well in a group setting, they are almost useless for homeschooling.

For many subjects, simply order the workbook, answer key, test, and test key. Order only what you need for an individual student, not an entire schoolroom.

8. <u>Shop back-to-school sales.</u> Since you likely know what school supplies you need yearly, stock up on basics at the return-to-school frenzy. Basic items sell at ridiculously low prices. Some of the items we buy often include lined paper, pencils, one- and two-inch notebooks, calculators, erasers, lined cards, and more. You know what you need for your family. Don't miss the opportunity to stock up on savings.

9. <u>Barter.</u> Why pay cash when you can barter? This is usually a win-win. When doing life together with your home-school community, stay aware of what others are using. Trade books with others for the school year that they need them for. Commonly, I trade science, math, and history resources with my girlfriends. This saves a tremendous amount of money, keeping costs down for everyone. Be sure to take good care of any borrowed materials. If damage occurs, replace the borrowed book with a new one.

10. <u>Keep it simple.</u> Overcomplicating the process of home-schooling can ensure failure. I speak from experience. Once you've formulated a plan for the school year, a review with an eye toward keeping it simple may encourage you to drop a few things off the list.

Create a proposal for evaluating the whole child. Then compile a schedule that includes each child and the family. Strategize how you will distribute your time between the children's school and your housekeeping responsibilities. Aim for empty spots in the day and week. You will need them for everyday surprises and for catching up. Planning saves money and ultimately time.

When aiming for savings as you launch into this school year, make a careful list of what you need. Shop locally and on Amazon, Facebook, eBay, and anywhere else you can save. Select dual-purpose tables and chairs. Pack coolers. Trade skills. Limit orders. Use the library; you already pay for it with your tax dollars. Shop back-to-school sales. Barter and trade. Lastly, don't forget to keep it simple.

Life is expensive. Surprise expenses are everywhere. Use these ten ways to save on your homeschooling needs.

Thanks to...

My heart is full of thanks to so many wonderful moms who have traveled this journey with me. A special thank-you to those of you who have done life with me on field trips, tutorials, speech and debate, AWANA, and Omnibus. In no particular order, these are some of the finest moms on the planet. What a privilege I have to know each of you! As you can see, it takes a community of mamas loving on their babies to do this job.

My sister, Daphne Vance Reichard

Kerri Pleben

Missy Kern

Kellye Stelling

Melody Yasi

Pat Wade

Linda Hobar

Teddi Reynolds

Katherine Barnhart

Michelle Wittman

Stephanie Moore

Trish Peel

Jenny Clayton

Laurie Sines

Erin Robbins

Jan Schulte

Kathy Ethridge

Teresa Pegrim

Patti Jelinek

Melissa Arman

Debbie Corley

Sherry Arnold

Kelley Landers

Jennifer Higgins

Sheila Battle

Kimberly Farley

Melissa Lovett

For those teaching dads who impacted us on this adventure, thank you.

Rick Jones

John Hodges

Terry Wade

Steve Ethridge

David Peel

For more encouragement and inspiration, sign up for updated blogs at www.nurturingmynest.com

Share your ideas for solutions to common homeschooling and homemaking dilemmas. Please communicate any questions or concerns to leah.grateful@gmail.com.

If you would like to have Leah speak at a women's event or a homeschool event, please contact her for a list of her popular talks.

NOTES

1   "Proportion of US Students in Private Schools Is 10 Percent and Declining," *Huffington Post*, accessed July 20, 2017, http://www.huffingtonpost.com/jack-jennings/proportion-of-us-students_b_2950948.html.

2   Simply Charlotte Mason.com, accessed July 20, 2017, https://simplycharlottemason.com/what-is-the-charlotte-mason-method/.

3   "Latin Influence on English," *Wikipedia*, accessed July 20, 2017, https://en.wikipedia.org/wiki/Latin_influence_in_English.

4   Thomas Jefferson, letter to Samuel H. Smith, Sept 21, 1814, in *L&B*, 14:190.

5   See in the above letter Jefferson's "Observations on the Transportation of the Monticello Library,"

6   Sheila Seifert, "Age Appropriate Chores," accessed on July 20, 2017, http://www.focusonthefamily.com/parenting/parenting-challenges/motivating-kids-to-clean-up/age-appropriate-chores.

7   Janice Campbell, "Carnival of Homeschooling: Making Time for Things that Matter," December 28, 2010 https://www.doingwhatmatters.com/?s=Carnival+of+homeschooling%3A++Making+time+for+things+that+matter.

8   Ibid.

9   Ibid., 3.

10 Ibid., 4.

11 Ibid., 13.

12 Ibid., 17.

13 Ibid., 19–20.

14 Janice Campbell, "How to Build a Quality Home Library Inexpensively,"
        accessed July 20, 2017, https://everyday-education.com/build-a-quality-home-library-without-breaking-your-budget/.

CPSIA information can be obtained
at www.ICGtesting.com
Printed in the USA
LVOW13s0208260318
571148LV00014B/274/P